# THE BRIDGE BOOK

## VOLUME 3 — FOR ADVANCED PLAYERS

### by Frank Stewart
### and Randall Baron

**Drawings by Jude Goodwin**

Published by
Devyn Press, Inc.
Louisville, Kentucky

# Dedications

To C.H.
—F.S.
To Mary, Devyn and Dustin.
—R.S.B.

# Acknowledgments

Grateful thanks to:
Betty Mattison for her patience and typesetting skills;
Pat Houington, Tony Lipka and Henry Francis for their editorial
assistance;
Izzy Ellis and V.B.I. for their cover photography;
also to Mary Black, Mimi Maier, and Bonnie Baron Pollack.

The reader is referred to as "he" to make the text more readable.

Printed in the United States of America.

Devyn Press Inc.
151 Thierman Lane
Louisville, KY 40207

ISBN 0-910791-55-4

# Table of Contents

# Preface

This book, the third in a series of four volumes, introduces the aspiring player to advanced ideas in bridge and challenges him to begin thinking like an expert. Although some of the material will do for a review, we encourage readers to brush up on Volumes 1 and 2, for Beginning and Intermediate players, before plunging into this one.

In *The Bridge Book, Vol. 3,* the bidding emphasis is on a sound grasp of the basics, coupled with good judgment and anticipation. (Little space is given to conventions and treatments, which are adequately covered in other books. However, in Chapter 10 we discuss the proper use of several of the most popular conventions.) In the play, we stress careful planning, counting and drawing inferences.

This book includes quizzes so that you may test your understanding of the material. Actual play has no peer as a learning experience, of course; try to put into practice what you learn as much as you can.

The rewards for those who master this stimulating pastime are well worth the effort. At the least, you will have a way of entertaining yourself and a means of making friends wherever you go. If you are more ambitious, tournament competition can lead to a world championship!

# Chapter 1

## PLANNING IN THE AUCTION

Thinking and planning will occupy us a lot in this book. When dummy comes down, a good declarer always plans as much of his play as possible before touching the first card. As declarer, you always count your sure winners and/or potential losers. You consider problems in timing, communication, avoidance, and so on. The spectrum over which the mind of a really fine declarer may range during the course of a hand is quite remarkable.

There is, however, a different kind of planning, which will concern us here — PLANNING IN THE AUCTION. Simple examples of this idea are common. For example, if you hold:

♠ x x
♡ K x x x
♢ J x x
♣ A Q x x

and partner opens 1 ♡, you may temporize with a 2 ♣ response, planning to support hearts at your next turn. On other occasions you may have to act like a chess player who looks several moves ahead — you may have to anticipate how the bidding will go so you will be comfortably placed at your *later* turns. Or you may have to make a bid that will give your side an edge in the play.

Perhaps the simplest instance of this type of anticipation is planning your *rebid* when you make your opening bid. A good player always knows what he will do over any response by his partner.

1. ♠ Q x      You are dealer. If you open 1 ♡, **what**
♡ A Q x x x      **is partner's most likely response?**
♢ K J x      1 ♠, right? You are now stuck for a
♣ A 10 x      rebid. *2 ♡* suggests a minimum with
long hearts; *3 ♡* promises a six-card suit and a more heart-oriented hand; *1 NT* shows fewer points; *2 NT* shows more. And you have no other suit to bid. Better to *open 1 NT* and avoid this trap. If your hearts and spades were reversed, you

might get away with a 1♠ opening. If partner responded in a new suit, it would be at the two level, and your chance of getting into big trouble would be remote. But with 2-5-3-3 pattern, you almost have to open 1 NT to avoid the looming rebid problems. And a 1 NT opening describes this hand well.

2.  a. ♠ A 10 x x x      b. ♠ K Q J 10 x
     ♡ x                 ♡ A x
     ◊ x x               ◊ x
     ♣ A K J x x        ♣ Q x x x x

   c. ♠ x x x x x      d. ♠ A K x x x
     ♡ A x               ♡ x
     ◊ x                ◊ A x
     ♣ A K Q 10 x      ♣ K Q 10 x x

The black 5-5 dilemma. Many authorities recommend always opening 1♠, and it is easy to understand this view. A 1♠ opening keeps the suit from getting lost, avoids the rebid problems that arise if partner responds 1 NT or 2♣ to your 1♣ opening, and is more preemptive. So, it seems better to open 1♠ if possible. However, think about what feature of your hand you want to emphasize in choosing an opening.

*CAREFULLY PLANNING YOUR BIDS WILL MAKE YOU A RESPECTED PARTNER AND FEARED OPPONENT.*

a. Open 1♣, bid and rebid spades. You cannot suppress the nice club suit, but you cannot bid it at the three level after a two level response to 1♠. Your hand is too minimum.*

b. Open 1♠ and just rebid the spades. Let the clubs go.

c. Open 1♣, rebid in spades if you can do that at the one level, then bid clubs again. Treat the spades like a four-card suit.

d. Open 1♠, intending to rebid 3♣ if partner responds in a red suit. You are strong enough to do this.

3.  a.  ♠ x
        ♡ K 9 x x
        ◇ A Q J x
        ♣ K J 9 x

    b.  ♠ Q x x x
        ♡ x
        ◇ A Q x x
        ♣ A J x x

    c.  ♠ J x x x
        ♡ A K Q x
        ◇ x
        ♣ A 10 x x

    d.  ♠ K x x x
        ♡ A J x x
        ◇ A 10 x x
        ♣ Q

4-4-4-1 woes. These are awkward hands. Trying to get all your suits into the bidding, find a fit if there is one, and keep from getting overboard in the process can be a real headache. Experts disagree about how you should begin to describe such hands. In some systems, there are even special bids of 2♣ or 2◇ to handle hands of this type.

a. Open 1◇. If you open 1♣ and partner says 1♠ (likely) or 1 NT, you are stuck.

b. Open 1◇. You cannot rebid if partner responds 1 NT to a 1♠ opening.

c. Most would open 1♣ routinely. You are okay unless partner responds 1 NT, in which case you must shoot out a pass (not so bad since he should have some diamonds; he didn't bid a major or raise clubs). A 1♡ opening isn't so bad, since you might reach a good 4-3 heart fit. But you stand to lose a club fit, and you will be in trouble if partner responds 2◇ to your 1♡.

d. Open 1◇. You will raise a major-suit response or pass 1 NT (partner is marked with at least four clubs). If he responds 2♣, you are willing to rebid 2 NT. Your singleton club *honor* may make the play in notrump a little easier.

———

*Partner should *not* assume you are 6-5 on this auction.

4.  ♠ x                          Pass. Your suits are ragged, and long
    ♡ A Q J                      card tricks will be hard to set up.
    ◇ K J x x                    Most of your values are in your short
    ♣ J x x x x                  suits. You have no length in the ma-
                                 jors. Also, if you open 1♣ and hear

1♠, you are stuck. Since this hand is borderline and there are potential
rebid problems, don't open the bidding.

5.  a.  ♠ A x                    b.  ♠ A x
        ♡ x x                        ♡ x x
        ◇ A K J x                    ◇ Q x x x
        ♣ J x x x x                  ♣ A K J x x

    c.  ♠ A Q                    d.  ♠ x x
        ♡ A 10                       ♡ A K x x
        ◇ Q x x x                    ◇ Q x
        ♣ J x x x x                  ♣ A K x x x

You have a near-minimum hand with a five-card suit and a higher-
ranking four-card suit. The problem is to bid *both* your suits without
reversing.

a.  Open 1◇, rebid 2♣ (or 1 NT, over a 1♡ response). Treat
    the diamonds like a five-card suit, the clubs like a four-bagger.
b.  Open 1♣, rebid 2♣ (or 1 NT, over a 1♡ response). The
    diamonds are too anemic to mention.
c.  Open 1♣, rebid 1 NT. This is best with so much of your high-
    card strength in your short suits.
d.  A real nightmare. If you open 1♣ and partner bids 1♠, you
    will either have to overbid (2♡, 2 NT) or underbid (2♣, 1 NT).
    Some players might *start* with 1 NT on this hand. An alter-
    native is to open 1♡. You can rebid 2♣ over a 1♠ or 1 NT
    response. And if partner says 2◇, you will be unlikely to get
    into much trouble with a 3♣ rebid.

6.  ♠ x x                        Treat this as a two-suiter. Open 1♡,
    ♡ A K Q x                    planning to rebid 2◇. You should
    ◇ A K x x                    not open 1 NT, because all of your
    ♣ x x x                      points are concentrated in the red suits.

8

7.  (a) ♠ Q         Open 1♣, intending to raise a red-suit
       ♡ A x x      response or rebid 2♣ over 1 NT. If
       ◊ K x x x    partner responds 1♠, however, rebid
       ♣ A J x x x   1 NT despite your unbalanced pattern.

While some hands with four diamonds and five clubs properly call for a 1◊ opening and a 2♣ rebid, this sequence has a dangerous drawback — it fails to limit opener's hand. If your hand is minimum, prefer an alternative sequence.

   (b) ♠ K Q x      Open 1♣. If partner bids diamonds or
       ♡ x            spades, you will raise, of course.
       ◊ K x x x    If he responds 1 NT, a 2♣ rebid will
       ♣ A J x x x   do. If he says 1♡, perhaps you should
                         treat your spades as a four-card suit,
                         making 1♠ your best rebid! This is
                         true only because your hand is un-
                         balanced, making it more desirable to
                         play in a suit.

8.  ♠ A Q        A 1 NT opening would appeal to many
    ♡ A 10       players because there is no good
    ◊ Q 9 x x x x   rebid after a 1◊ opening and a major-
    ♣ K J x        suit response. You would prefer bet-
                    ter diamonds to rebid 3◊.

9.  ♠ A Q x x     This huge 4-4-4-1 is a bad hand for
    ♡ x           Standard bidding. You must risk a
    ◊ A K x x    1♣ opening. You must keep the bid-
    ♣ A K Q x    ding low so you will have a chance
                    to find a fit. If you open with a forcing

two-bid, the auction may get too high (past 3 NT, for instance) too fast.

10. ♠ A K J x     There are *two passes to you.* You
    ♡ Q x        have two Quick Tricks so you can
    ◊ Q 10 x x    open, and you can comfortably pass
    ♣ x x x       any response. That being so, you may
                    as well take advantage of the preemp-

tive and lead-directing effects of a 1♠ opening.

11. ♠ Q J x x

    ♡ x

    ◇ A x x

    ♣ A K x x x

*Partner opens* 1♡. Since you have plenty of ammunition, you can show your suits in their natural order. Respond 2♣, planning to bid spades next when partner makes his expected 2♡ rebid. But . . .

12. ♠ K J x x

    ♡ x x

    ◇ K x

    ♣ Q J x x x

Respond 1♠. If you bid 2♣, then 2♠ as on the last hand, you fail to limit your strength and risk getting too high. Since you plan to show only one suit, it should be the major.

13. ♠ A Q 10 x

    ♡ K J x x

    ◇ x x x

    ♣ x x

Respond 1♠ and raise hearts next. You must temporize at your first turn because no immediate heart raise is right. (Even if you play *limit raises,* and a double raise is invitational and not forcing, a 1♠ response, showing where your side strength lies, is superior to 3♡. Partner may be able to make a better decision about game chances if he knows you have good spades. A limit raise should show prime values, good trumps and good shape.)

---

14. ♠ x

    ♡ A x

    ◇ A K J x x x

    ♣ A 10 x x

You opened 1◇, partner responded 1♠. 3◇ is the straightforward rebid, but 2♣ is more flexible. You plan to bid diamonds again at your next turn. To show a strongish 6-4, you bid your six-card suit, then your four-card suit, then the six-card suit again. If weaker, rebid 2◇.

---

15. ♠ x x

    ♡ Q 9 x x x

    ◇ K x

    ♣ A Q 10 x

Partner opens 1◇, you respond 1♡, he rebids 1♠. Bid 2 NT, a game invitation. There is little reason to bid 2♣. Even if partner could take a heart preference, you would still want to play notrump with your good clubs and bad hearts. And if partner were to bid 2 NT over 2♣, you would have to guess whether to bid three. Your partnership will be better placed if you limit the hand now with a 2 NT rebid.

16.　♠ A x
　　　♡ A Q 10 x x
　　　◇ Q x
　　　♣ A K J x

You open 1♡, partner responds 1 NT. You will rebid 3♣, of course. But if partner takes a heart preference, bid 3 NT, suggesting semi-balanced pattern despite your heart and club bids.

Partner is free to return to hearts if he wants.

---

17.　♠ A Q x x x
　　　♡ x
　　　◇ A K x
　　　♣ A J x x

Partner opens 1♡. Slam is possible, but the best strain is in doubt. It could be any of the four suits or notrump. Nowadays, good players avoid a jump shift if the proper strain is in doubt.

Respond 1♠, leaving plenty of room to explore for the best fit without reaching very far past game if slam begins to look doubtful.

---

18.　♠ K x x
　　　♡ A Q J x x
　　　◇ A J x
　　　♣ x x

RHO opens 1♣. Overcall 1♡. You are by no means strong enough to double and then bid hearts, so a double stands to miss a 5-3 heart fit. If you overcall and the bidding continues 2♣

- Pass - Pass, you can double and describe your hand accurately.

19.　♠ A Q 10 x x
　　　♡ A x x
　　　◇ K Q x x x
　　　♣ —

RHO opens 1♣. Overcall 1♠, intending to bid diamonds next. If you start with a takeout double on a two-suiter, competition may keep you from showing the nature of your hand.

20.　♠ Q x x x
　　　♡ x
　　　◇ A K J x x
　　　♣ x x x

LHO, vulnerable, opens 1♡. Your partner jumps to 2♠ (weak), and RHO bids 3♡. 4◇ by you will direct a lead and help partner decide what to do if the enemy goes on to 5♡ over your eventual 4♠ sacrifice.

# SUMMARY

Planning the play as declarer or defender is a well known skill at bridge. A lesser known but equally important skill is *PLANNING IN THE AUCTION.*

During the auction, you may have to:

| | |
|---|---|
| 1. | Decide which features of your hand are most important. |
| 2. | Plan how to show your suits and describe your features economically. |
| 3. | Anticipate a rebid with your choice of an opening bid or a response. |
| 4. | Foresee competition by the opponents. |
| 5. | Make a bid that will give your side an edge in the *play*. |

## TEST YOUR COMPREHENSION OF THE MATERIAL IN THIS CHAPTER:

1. ♠ J x
   ♡ K Q x x x
   ◇ A 10 x
   ♣ A Q x

   You are dealer. What is your opening bid?

2. ♠ A K Q 10
   ♡ J x x x x
   ◇ K J x
   ♣ x

   You are dealer. What is your opening bid?

3. ♠ Q
   ♡ K 10 x x
   ◇ A Q x x
   ♣ K x x x

   You are dealer. What is your opening bid?

4. ♠ x
   ♡ K 10 x x x
   ◇ A J x x
   ♣ Q J x

   You are in third seat after two passes. What is your action?

5. ♠ A K J 10    Partner opens 1♣. What is your first
   ♡ Q x x x      response and how do you plan the
   ◇ x x          auction?
   ♣ K x x

6. ♠ A Q x x    You open 1◇, and partner responds
   ♡ x           1♠. Where do you go from here?
   ◇ A K J x x
   ♣ A J x

7. ♠ A Q x      You open 1◇, and partner responds
   ♡ A x x       1♠. What are your plans?
   ◇ A K J x x x
   ♣ x

8. ♠ x          You open 1◇, and partner responds
   ♡ A K x       1♠. How do you continue?
   ◇ K 10 x x x x
   ♣ A Q x

9. ♠ Q 10 x     Partner opens 1◇, RHO doubles.
   ♡ K J x x     What are your plans?
   ◇ J x x
   ♣ Q x x

10. ♠ K x x     You open 1♣, partner responds 1♠,
    ♡ A x x      RHO doubles. What are your plans?
    ◇ x
    ♣ K Q J x x x

11. ♠ —         Left-hand opponent opens 4♠ (neither
    ♡ A Q 10 x x  side vulnerable), passed to you. What
    ◇ A K x x x x are your plans?
    ♣ x x

12. ♠ x         RHO opens 1◇ (both sides vulner-
    ♡ A J 10 x   able). What are your plans?
    ◇ K Q x x
    ♣ A J 9 x

13

13. ♠ J 10 x x          LHO opens 1 ♡, partner doubles, RHO
    ♡ Q 10 x x        passes. What are your plans?
    ◊ K x
    ♣ Q J x

14   ♠ x x             Your LHO opens 1♡ after three
    ♡ x              passes. Partner comes in with 1 ♠, and
    ◊ J 9 x x x x    RHO cuebids 2 ♠, showing a good
    ♣ A Q 10 x      heart raise. They are vulnerable, you
                       are not. What is your action?

15. ♠ A x            You open 1 ♡, LHO overcalls 1 ♠,
    ♡ A Q 9 x x x   partner raises to 2 ♡, RHO jumps
    ◊ x              to 3 ♠ (preemptive). What is your
    ♣ A x x x       action?

16. ♠ K J x x x      Partner opens 1 ◊, you respond 1 ♠.
    ♡ —             Partner rebids 2 ◊. What is your
    ◊ 9 x x        action?
    ♣ K 10 x x x

# SOLUTIONS

1. Open 1 NT, avoiding the potential rebid problems after a 1 ♡ opening.

2. Open 1 ♠. If you open 1 ♡ and hear a 1 NT response, you will be stuck for a rebid.

3. Open 1 ♣. If partner responds 1 ♠, you are willing to rebid 1 NT despite your singleton ♠Q. The play may be easier in notrump, and this rebid has the benefit of limiting your hand quickly. If partner insists on spades, your queen will help solidify his suit. If partner responds 1 NT to 1 ♣, passing with a singleton spade *honor* won't be so bad.

4. Pass. If you open 1 ♡ and hear 1 ♠ from partner, you cannot leave him there. But if you bid again, you confirm a sound opening bid. You lack the defensive values to open and you are not anxious for a heart lead if you defend. So why open?

5. Respond 1 ♠, treating your suit as a five-bagger. If partner does not raise directly, you will bid hearts next, inviting him to take a spade preference with three-card support. Your spades are so strong that a spade contract on a 4-3 fit could be best.

6. Jump to 3 ♣, intending to bid 4 ♠ next. You show a raise to 4 ♠ with shortness in the suit you don't bid. A direct 4 ♠ would suggest a balanced hand.

7. Bid 2 ♡, planning to show your spade support next. This sequence suggests strength and club shortness. Don't worry about a heart raise from partner. He won't raise your second suit with fewer than four cards, and if he has four hearts, he must have at least *five* spades. (He would usually respond 1 ♡ with four cards in each major.)

8. Rebid 2 ♣. No diamond rebid is exactly right. You would prefer a better suit to jump in diamonds. If partner raises clubs, you can bid notrump (or hearts, completing a description of your pattern). If he rebids spades, you bid notrump. If he takes a diamond preference, you probably bid hearts next and see if that excites him.

9. Bid 1 NT. Make the bid that best describes your hand in an auction that has turned competitive.

10. Bid 2 ♣. If you don't get a club rebid in now, there may never be a convenient time. You can show your spade support later.

11. Bid 4 NT, for takeout. You expect partner to bid clubs, whereupon you will ease out to diamonds. Now he knows you have diamonds *and hearts*, since you would have just bid diamonds directly with a one-suiter.

12. Pass. You cannot double with no spade tolerance, and the only alternative is an overcall in a four-card suit. You expect LHO to respond in spades, and if opener then rebids 1 NT, 2 ♠, 2 ◇ or even 2 ♣, you can double and describe your hand well.

13. Respond 1 NT. This is not a bad action anyway, with all those secondary values and the double heart stopper. But an added advantage is that if there is competition (say it goes 2 ◇ on your left, pass, pass) you can then bid 2 ♠, playing in either that contract or 2 NT as partner prefers. You may miss a good notrump contract if you respond in spades first.

14. Frank Stewart held this hand in a team match and risked 3 ♣. As he expected, the opponents went on and bid their heart game. But partner now led the ♣K from K-x! This was the only lead to give the defense a chance, and the contract was duly defeated.

15. No guarantees, but you might bid 4 ◇, hoping to get partner off to a diamond lead if the eventual contract is 4 ♠ doubled. If his only fast entry is the ♡ K, an initial diamond lead may be vital.

16. This hand is taken from Terence Reese's *Develop Your Bidding Judgment*. Reese recommends a pass. There is a case for raising 2 ◇ to 3 ◇ to keep the opponents from coming in with hearts, but Reese's point is that the opponents will probably find *hearts stacked against them* — they may go down badly if they get to the four level. Reese plans to pull to 3 ◇ if LHO balances with 2 ♡ and partner doubles; or go to 4 ◇ if partner bids 3 ◇ by himself, and the opponents compete to 3 ♡.

# Chapter 2

## COUNTING

By now, you know how important techniques of *counting* are in winning bridge. This thread runs through the fabric of the game.

In this chapter we will talk about *counting* by *declarer*. Of course, as an experienced player, you *always* observe declarer's most important occasion for counting. You COUNT YOUR TRICKS in planning the play, and you do this *before* you play the first card. You note sure winners, potential losers or both. This kind of counting often gives you the perspective you need to play the hand successfully.

♠ J 10 3
♡ A Q
♢ K 6 4 2
♣ A K Q 2

♠ K 7 4
♡ 5 4 3
♢ A J 10 5
♣ 5 4 3

You, South, are declarer in 3 NT. West leads the ♠6. You play dummy's jack, winning; East follows with the nine, suggesting that West led from a five-card suit headed by the ace and queen. **What would you play to trick two?**

You have one trick in the bag and six more in top cards. If you can bring in four diamond tricks, you will make the game; but if you take only three diamonds, you will need either the heart finesse to work or the clubs to split evenly.

Of course, this is an *avoidance* position. Bad things will happen if *East* gains the lead and returns a spade through your king. You would rather not rely on the heart finesse, and for the same reason, you will finesse diamonds *into West*. Suppose you lead a diamond to your jack at trick two, and it loses. What would you do if West now returned a *heart?* You would have to decide right away whether to take the heart finesse or rely on a favorable club break. A heart return would deprive you of one of your options.

The correct play is clear. You should cash dummy's high clubs after winning the opening lead. By finding out how many club tricks are available, you will know whether the heart finesse will be a necessary evil if the diamond finesse loses. You preserve *all* your chances.

Declarer also may find it helpful to count the opponents' high-card *POINTS.* We will talk more about this later.

The type of counting we discuss here is:

### COUNTING THE DISTRIBUTION OF
### THE CONCEALED HANDS

To begin, let's look at a tough hand that would be almost impossible to make *without* counting the opponents' distribution.

1.
    ♠ J 10 8 6
    ♡ 6 5
    ◊ K 10 7
    ♣ A K Q 4

    ♠ A K Q 9 4
    ♡ A Q 4
    ◊ J 9 6 4
    ♣ 3

You reach an optimistic 6♠. The opening lead is the ♡7, solving one of your problems. East plays the ♡K, and you win. You draw trumps in two rounds, cash your ♡A, East following with the ten, and ruff your low heart in dummy, as East shows out, pitching a diamond. **How many hearts did East have?** *Two,* **so West had how many hearts?** *Six* hearts. Suppose you continue with three top clubs, throwing two diamonds. Both opponents follow. You lead the fourth club, intending to ruff and make a diamond play, but East shows out, pitching a second diamond. **How should you play now?**

East had only *three* clubs, **so how many did West have?** *Five.* **What was West's distribution?** Two spades, six hearts, five clubs . . . that's 13 cards, so West has no diamonds. If you ruff the fourth club and lead a diamond, you will be swiftly down. **What is the alternative?**

Right, you *discard* your next-to-last diamond on the fourth club. West wins, but he must lead a club or a heart; either way, you ruff in dummy and get rid of your last diamond!

Many less-experienced players consider *reconstructing the concealed hands* as something for experts only. In principle, this is a *simple* process, well within the reach of *anyone*.

To succeed at counting the hands, all you need are:

| | |
|---|---|
| 1. | A little concentration |
| 2. | A little practice |
| 3. | The ability to *count to 13.* |

Counting distribution is based on two obvious facts:

> 1. There are 13 cards in each *suit*.
> 2. There are 13 cards in each *hand*.

If you know that West had three spades, and you and dummy had four each, then East must have two spades. There are 13 cards in each *suit*.

If you know that West had three spades, four hearts and two clubs, then West must have had *four diamonds*. There are 13 cards in each *hand*.

The only problem is paying close attention to the play. That's where concentration and practice come in. Let's look at some hands and drill on counting the opponents' distribution. This will give you part of the practice you need.

2.
      ♠ J 8 4
      ♡ A 5 4 3 2
      ◇ 5 4
      ♣ K J 3

      ♠ K Q 9 5 3
      ♡ 7 6
      ◇ K Q 6
      ♣ A 10 5

You and partner have overbid, landing in 4♠ (but if you play the dummy well, you can afford to be aggressive in the bidding). West leads the ♡8, and you win dummy's ace. You lead a diamond to your queen immediately, since you may need to ruff your third diamond. West wins the ◇A, cashes the ♡K, dropping East's queen, and continues with a heart. East discards a club, and you ruff. You continue with the ◇K and another diamond, ruffed in dummy. Both opponents follow. Next you lead the ♠J from dummy. It wins the trick, as the opponents follow. So you lead another spade. East wins the ace, as West follows, and leads a diamond. You ruff with your ♠9, and West follows. So you play off your ♠K, drawing trumps. West follows, while East discards a club. All hands are now down to three cards. **How should you guess the club suit?**

Let's look at the evidence, suit by suit.

Spades . . . . . . . . . . West had *three.*   East had *two.*
Hearts . . . . . . . . . . . West had *four.*   East had *two.*
Diamonds . . . . . . . . West had *four.*   East had *four.*
Clubs? You can work it out if you can count to 13.
                    West had *two.*   East had *five.*

The odds are *5 to 2* that East has any particular one of the missing clubs, including the queen. So you take your make-or-break finesse through *East.* (A good declarer will, of course, consider many factors in making a decision like this. He may count the *high-card points* the opponents show in the play. On this hand, the evidence of high-card points is inconclusive, and declarer must rely on his *distributional* count alone.)

In the first two hands we discussed, the information declarer needed to get a count fell into his lap routinely during the course of play. But on many hands declarer must actively seek to get a count.

3.                    ♠ Q 3 2
                     ♡ Q 8 5 3
                     ◊ A 10 2
                     ♣ K 3 2

                     ♠ J 7 4
                     ♡ A K J 6 4
                     ◊ K J 4
                     ♣ A 7

You are declarer in 4 ♡ after West overcalled in spades. West leads the ♠A and follows with the king. East discards and ruffs the third spade. The ♣10 is returned, and you win the ace. You draw three rounds of trumps, finding that East got his ruff with a singleton trump. Now, before you make your diamond play, lead the ♣K and ruff dummy's club. You might get some useful information. As it happens, West follows to all three rounds of clubs, so your diamond guess is now a sure thing. West had *six* spades, *three* hearts and at least *three* clubs, *so he has at most one diamond.* (Remember, he had only 13 cards.) Lead a diamond to the ace. If the queen does not appear from West, a finesse of your ◊J is bound to work.

21

Sometimes, you must do a *lot* of digging to get the information you need.

4.
&#9824; 8 5
&#9825; K 10 3
&#9826; K 10 5 4
&#9827; A K 3 2

&#9824; J 7 2
&#9825; A J 7 2
&#9826; A Q J 8 3
&#9827; 7

| South | West | North | East |
|-------|------|-------|------|
| 1 &#9826; | 1 &#9824; | 3 &#9826; | Pass |
| 4 &#9826; | Pass | 5 &#9826; | (All Pass) |

West leads the &#9824;K. East overtakes with the ace and returns a spade to West's ten. When the &#9824;Q is led, you ruff with dummy's &#9826; 10, and East shows out. Keep in mind that East had only *two* spades, and West had *six*. You draw trumps in two rounds. East had *two* diamonds, West had *two*. **How would you continue?**

You would like to know the heart distribution. You know eight of West's original 13 cards. If you could find out how many clubs West had, you would know about the hearts. Play the &#9827;A and &#9827;K and trump a club. Your purpose is to find out how many clubs everyone had. Say that both opponents follow to three rounds of clubs. So you're getting close to an answer. You know that West had six spades, two diamonds and at least three clubs. That's 11 of his original 13 cards.

Now you can return to dummy with the &#9826;K and ruff the fourth club. No matter what happens, you will get a *complete count*. Suppose that both East and West follow to the fourth round of clubs. Your problems are over! West had *six* spades, *two* diamonds, *four* clubs and . . . *one* heart. Play a heart to the king to see which heart West had. If it's not the queen, you can finesse against East. Your finesse must work.

5.

♠ Q 9 5 3
♡ A J 8 4
◇ A Q 3
♣ 8 7

♠ A K J 6 4
♡ K 9 3 2
◇ 8 5
♣ Q 4

You are declarer in 4 ♠ after West overcalled in clubs. West leads the ♣A and ♣K, with East playing the three and six. West then shifts to a diamond. You finesse the queen, losing to East, and a diamond is returned and won by dummy's ace. You draw three rounds of trumps, ending in dummy. West had a singleton spade, East had three. Now you ruff dummy's last diamond. West shows out on this trick, discarding a club. **How should you play the hearts?**

You know West had *one* spade and *two* diamonds. He had *at least five* clubs for his overcall, but *no more than six* clubs, since East failed to play high-low on the club leads. So how many hearts does West have? At least *four*. Play your ♡ K and follow with a heart, intending to finesse dummy's *eight*.

6.

♠ Q 7 3 2
♡ A K
◇ A J 2
♣ 6 5 4 3

♠ 5
♡ Q J 10 9 5 3
◇ Q 10 4 3
♣ K J

West opened 1 ♠, but you and partner took over and got to 4 ♡.

West leads the ♠ A. East plays the ♠ 4, and West shifts to a trump. You win and lead a club to your jack. West produces the queen and plays a second trump, to which East follows. You lead another club to your king and West's ace. This time West returns a club to East's ten, which you ruff. You draw the last trump, West discarding a spade. Now a low diamond is led to dummy's jack. East plays low.

**What should you do at this point?**

You can afford to ruff dummy's last club, hoping to get a count. Say East discards a spade and West follows. So you know that West had *four* clubs and *two* hearts. He surely had *five* spades to open the bidding in that suit. So you can now lead another *low* diamond, expecting West's king to pop up. Note that you would have to lose a trick to East's 9-8-x-x if you led one of your diamond honors.

Our last hand shows how counting can keep you from adopting a hopeless line of play.

7.
    ♠ 6 5
    ♡ 7 5 4
    ◇ K Q J 5 4
    ♣ A 7 4

    ♠ A K 9 8 4 3
    ♡ K 8
    ◇ A 2
    ♣ 8 5 3

East opened 3♡, you risked a 3♠ overcall, and partner raised you to 4♠. West leads the ♡Q. East wins the ace and returns a low heart, which West ruffs low. You win the ♣Q return in dummy, and East plays the king. When you cash your high trumps, West discards a club on the second round. **What should you do now?**

Don't forget to *count*. East had *seven* hearts, *three* spades and *at least one* club. Therefore, he had *no more than two* diamonds. You may be thinking of playing diamonds right away, hoping to throw your club losers away before East can ruff in, but you should forget it. It's impossible. Your only hope is that East had the singleton ♣K. So you must go ahead and give him his trump trick and hope he has no club left to return. Then you can run your diamonds without being interrupted.

# SUMMARY

Counting the defenders' distribution may help determine a good line of play or locate a crucial honor. To succeed at counting the missing hands, all you need is:

1. A little CONCENTRATION
2. A little PRACTICE
3. The ability to COUNT TO 13

*This technique is not for experts only.* It is based on simple ideas and therefore is within reach of any player.

Counting distribution is based on two obvious facts:

1. Each suit has 13 cards.
2. Each hand has 13 cards.

If West had three spades, and you and dummy had four each, East must have had two spades. *There are 13 cards in each suit.*

If West had three spades, four hearts and two clubs, then West must have had four diamonds. *There are 13 cards in each hand.*

All you must do is pay attention to the play of the cards and remember what happens.

*TRY THESE 6 PROBLEMS TO TEST YOUR COUNTING COMPREHENSION.*

## TEST YOUR COMPREHENSION OF THE MATERIAL IN THIS CHAPTER:

1.
     ♠ A 3 2
     ♡ A J 3
     ◇ A J 10 4
     ♣ 4 3 2

     ♠ K 4
     ♡ K Q 9 8 2
     ◇ K 3 2
     ♣ Q 8 7

You are declarer in 4 ♡. West leads the ♣ 9. East wins the king and ace, and returns a club that West ruffs. You win the spade return and draw trumps. East follows to four rounds. Next you play the ♠ A and ruff a spade, both opponents following. How do you play diamonds?

2.
     ♠ Q 3 2
     ♡ 2
     ◇ K Q 3 2
     ♣ Q 10 9 4 2

     ♠ A J 6 5 4
     ♡ 3
     ◇ 5 4
     ♣ A K J 7 3

East opened 1 ♡, you chose to overcall 2 ♣, West bid 4 ♡, North raised to 5 ♣, everyone passed. West leads the ◇ J. East wins the ace, cashes the ♡ K and returns a diamond to dummy. You ruff a diamond, as East shows out, and draw two rounds of trumps, finding East with a singleton. How do you play the spades?

3.
    ♠ Q 10 8
    ♡ Q 3 2
    ◇ A J 2
    ♣ A K 3 2

    ♠ A K J 9 7
    ♡ 6 5 4
    ◇ K 10 3
    ♣ 5 4

 You are declarer in 4♠. West leads the ♡J, and the defenders take the first three tricks in that suit and exit with a trump. You win and draw a second round, both opponents following. Now you play the high clubs and ruff a club. West shows out on the third club. When you draw the last outstanding trump, West shows out. How do you play the diamonds?

4.
    ♠ Q 5
    ♡ 4 3 2
    ◇ K Q 10 4
    ♣ A Q 9 2

    ♠ A 9 3
    ♡ K J 7 6 5
    ◇ A 3
    ♣ K 4 3

 You are declarer in 3 NT. West leads the ♣4, and dummy's queen wins. At trick two you elect to lead a heart to your king. West wins the ace and returns the ♠2 to East's jack. You duck and win the third spade. Both opponents follow to three top diamonds, but no jack falls. Next you lead a club to the queen and a club back to your king. Both opponents follow, with East playing the ten on the second round. When you lead a third club toward dummy, West plays low. Do you finesse dummy's nine or play the ♣A?

5.                 ♠ A 2
                    ♡ K Q 2
                    ◇ 8 7 6 5 4
                    ♣ A Q 2

                 ♠ K Q J 3
                    ♡ A 10 4 3
                    ◇ A 9
                    ♣ K 4 3

You are declarer in 6 NT. West leads the ♣J, which you win. What do you lead at trick two?

6.                 ♠ 5 4 3 2
                    ♡ Q 9 8
                    ◇ A 9 2
                    ♣ 4 3 2

                 ♠ A K
                    ♡ A K J 10 7
                    ◇ Q 8 4 3
                    ♣ J 5

You are declarer in 4 ♡ after West overcalled in clubs. West leads the ♣K. East overtakes with the ace and returns a club to West's queen. You ruff a third club as East discards a spade. You draw trumps, finding West with three, East with two. Both opponents follow to the ♠A and ♠K. How do you play the diamonds?

# SOLUTIONS

1. East had five clubs, four hearts and at least three spades. Therefore, he had at most one diamond. Play the ◊ K and a diamond to dummy's jack.

2. East had one club and two diamonds. He had at least six hearts (he would have opened 1♣ with 5-5 in the majors) but probably no more than six, else he might have bid 5♡. So East had at least three spades and probably four. You cannot hope for ♣Kx onside, so lead a spade to your ace, hoping that West has the singleton king. This is your only chance.

3. West had three or four hearts, two clubs and two spades. So he had at least five diamonds. The odds greatly favor taking the diamond finesse through West.

4. West had at least three diamonds and presumably five spades. Say that you play the ♣A, and East shows out. That would mean West had four clubs, and therefore he had a singleton ♡ A. You could lead a heart from dummy toward your queen safely. (East could win and cash the ◊ J, but he would have to give you the last trick.) You might go down if you finesse dummy's ♣9 and lose to the jack, but you can't go wrong by *winning* the third club.

5. *Duck* a diamond. This is a sure loser anyway. Your aim is to play as many tricks as possible before you attack hearts, hoping to get some sort of count. For instance, if you find West with five clubs, four spades and two diamonds, you will know what to do in hearts.

6. To get out for one diamond loser, you would normally have to hope for 3-3 diamonds with the king onside. That is impossible here. West had six clubs, three hearts and at least two spades, so diamonds can't be 3-3. Luckily, there is an alternative. Lead a diamond to the nine, playing West for K-x. You will lose this trick to East's jack or ten, but the king will come up on the next diamond lead, letting you win and continue by finessing to the eight in your hand.

BE AN ETHICAL PLAYER. ALWAYS DOUBLE IN THE SAME
TONE OF VOICE, SO THAT THE OTHER THREE PLAYERS
AT THE TABLE CANNOT DRAW AN INFERENCE
ABOUT YOUR HAND.

# Lesson 3

## DOUBLES AND REDOUBLES

The *double* and the *redouble* have many possible applications. In this chapter we look at some of their proper uses and learn to improve our *judgment* in applying them.

I. DOUBLES FOR PENALTY

Of course, you love to double the opponents and extract a penalty in four figures. Therefore, perhaps, we should emphasize the times when a penalty double is *not* well judged.

*DON'T DOUBLE:*

1. When the opponents bid to a high contract and you have general high-card strength. If they have found a suit, they probably have good distribution to make up for their lack of high cards. Some of your high cards will surely be ruffed. If they are in notrump, they may have a long suit to run — you will have trouble keeping a guard to all your high cards and may be subject to various squeezes and endplays. Even worse, your double may guide declarer and help him make a contract that otherwise would have failed.

2. When they voluntarily bid a slam in a suit and you have two aces. They should have a void suit and one of your aces won't cash. Furthermore, if this is the case, they may redouble!

3. When an opponent has made a bid that is forcing and may get his side into even deeper trouble. (However, you may need to double to direct partner's lead in some situations.)

4. When the opponents have reached the only contract you can beat. You will be sorry if they run to a more successful contract.

| South | West | North | East |
|-------|------|-------|------|
|       |      |       | 1 ♠  |
| Pass  | 2 ♠  | Pass  | 3 ♡  |
| Pass  | 4 ♡  | Pass  | Pass |
| ?     |      |       |      |

You, South, hold:   ♠ 6 5
                          ♡ Q J 10 7 5
                          ◇ K 8 5
                          ♣ 10 7 5

You must pass. You expect to set 4 ♡, but if you double and they run to 4 ♠, who knows what the outcome will be?

5.     When an opponent overcalls, with a stack in his suit but nothing else.

| South | West | North | East |
|-------|------|-------|------|
|       |      | 1 ♠   | 2 ◇  |
| ?     |      |       |      |

You, South, hold:   ♠ 8 6
                          ♡ 8 7 4
                          ◇ K J 10 7 6 4
                          ♣ J 7

You must *pass*. East won't make 2 ◇, but the problem is that there may be more bidding. If you double and the opponents run to, say, 2 ♡, partner may double that, expecting you to have more in high cards. Pass for now, and if partner can reopen with a double, you can pass again for penalty.

6.     With length, but not strength, in trumps. You may be *endplayed in trumps* and forced to lead from your trump holding.

7.     When the hand appears to be a *freak* and both sides have a *double fit*. You may do better in the long run to be declarer on such hands. You have much to gain and comparatively little to lose.

8.  When the opponents are *cuebidding* to slam. On some occasions you may direct an effective opening lead, but on others you give the opponents extra options in the bidding (pass, redouble) and help them judge their prospects. If you may be the opening leader yourself or if partner occasionally leads the right suit with no help, refrain from doubling.

The best time to spring a double on unsuspecting opponents is *when you know something they don't.* Look at this example of an *inferential penalty double:*

| South | West | North | East |
|-------|------|-------|------|
|       |      |       | 1 ♣  |
| Pass  | 1 ♠  | Pass  | 1 NT |
| Pass  | 2 NT | Pass  | 3 NT |
| ?     |      |       |      |

You, South, hold:

♠ 7
♡ J 9 6 4
◊ Q J 10 8
♣ K J 9 6

You should double. They aren't going to make it. The auction indicates that they have no extra high-card strength, and you know their key suits are splitting badly. In addition, you have a good attacking lead in the ◊ Q. True, declarer will suspect that your double is based partly on club strength, but he probably won't be able to do much about it. A double may collect a huge bundle of points.

| South | West | North | East |
|-------|------|-------|------|
|       |      |       | 1 ♠  |
| Pass  | 2 ♠  | Pass  | 3 ♠  |
| Pass  | 4 ♠  | Pass  | Pass |
| ?     |      |       |      |

You, South, hold:

♠ Q J 10 8
♡ 7 6 4
◊ 7 6 3
♣ 9 6 4

Believe it or not, this is another excellent double. Once again, you can tell that the opponents have nothing extra, and they are running into a bad trump break this time. They may be hoping for no spade losers and they have two. This double could pay extra dividends against a naive declarer who will play you for the missing high cards your partner holds.

| South | West | North | East |
|-------|------|-------|------|
|       |      |       | 1 ♡  |
| Pass  | 2 ♣  | Pass  | 3 ♣  |
| Pass  | 3 ♡  | Pass  | 4 ♡  |
| ?     |      |       |      |

You, South, hold:  ♠ 10 8 5 4
                               ♡ A 4
                               ◊ 9 7 5
                               ♣ A 8 6 4

Double. Partner is marked with club shortness on the auction, and you can visualize the defense: the ♣ A and another club, ruffed, and another club ruff when you win your ♡ A. Partner may have another high-card trick, and that will be two down!

## II. DOUBLES FOR TAKEOUT

Three basic conditions must be met for a double to be interpreted as **FOR TAKEOUT**:

---

1. Partner must not have bid, doubled or redoubled.
2. The level must be low. Doubles of openings above 4 ♡ and doubles of contracts the opponents reach in several rounds of bidding (as well as doubles of notrump openings) are for PENALTY.
3. A double of a suit bid is for TAKEOUT only if made at the first opportunity to double that suit. (An exception occurs when the opponents stop low in their fit and you *reopen* the bidding with a double.

---

Let's look at some bidding sequences and decide whether a double should be for PENALTY or for TAKEOUT.

| | South | West | North | East | |
|---|---|---|---|---|---|
| 1. | 1♡ | Pass | 2♡ | Double | TAKEOUT |
| 2. | 1♡ | Pass | 2♡ | Pass | |
| | Pass | Double | | | TAKEOUT (reopening) |
| 3. | 1♡ | Pass | 1♠ | 1 NT | |
| | Double | | | | PENALTY |
| 4. | 1♡ | Pass | 1♠ | Pass | |
| | 2♣ | Double | | | TAKEOUT |
| 5. | 3♡ | Pass | Pass | Double | TAKEOUT |
| 6. | 1♣ | Pass | 1♡ | Double | TAKEOUT |
| 7. | 1♡ | 1♠ | Double | | PENALTY, |
| | | | in the absence of any conventional understanding. | | |
| 8. | 1♡ | 2♣ | 2♠ | Pass | |
| | Pass | Double | | | TAKEOUT |
| 9. | 1 NT | Double | | | PENALTY |
| 10. | 1 NT | 2♠ | Double | | PENALTY |
| 11. | 1♡ | Double | 1♠ | Double | PENALTY |
| 12. | 4♠ | Double | | | PENALTY |
| 13. | 1♣ | Double | Pass | 1♡ | |
| | Double* | | | | *TAKEOUT |
| 14. | 1 NT | 2♡ | Pass | Pass | |
| | Double | | | | TAKEOUT (*in front of* the 2♡ bidder) |
| 15. | 1 NT | Pass | Pass | 2♡ | |
| | Double | | | | PENALTY (*behind* the 2♡ bidder) |
| 16. | 4♡ | Pass | Pass | Double | TAKEOUT |
| | | (but often passed if West does not have spades) | | | |

## III. LEAD-DIRECTING DOUBLES

Certain penalty doubles are intended not so much to increase the size of the penalty, but to give a better chance to defeat the contract. They do this by conventionally requesting a *specific lead*.

1. Against 3 NT:

    If partner has bid a suit and doubles 3 NT, lead his suit.
    If you have bid a suit and you double 3 NT, partner must lead your suit.
    If you have bid a suit and partner doubles 3 NT, lead your own suit. Partner has help for you.
    If you both have bid a suit, the doubler requests the lead of his own suit.

    If your side has not bid:

    Lead dummy's first-bid suit, if dummy has bid a suit. (However, if dummy *rebid* this suit and is known to have length and strength, partner's double may not ask for a specific lead.)
    Against an auction like 1 NT - Pass - 3 NT - Double, make an *unusual* lead, usually your *shortest* suit. Partner has a good suit, such as A-K-Q-x-x-x, and hopes you will lead it.

2. Against voluntarily-bid games and slams that the opponents reach on *strong-sounding auctions:*

    A double requests an unusual lead. *Frequently, this will be the lead of dummy's first-bid suit,* which you probably would not consider without the double. If partner doubles a suit contract in this situation, he may have a side void, so you often lead your longest suit, hoping he will ruff. Do *not* lead trumps, an unbid suit, or partner's suit if he bid a suit. (Doubles of contracts the opponents reach on *weak*-sounding auctions do not suggest a particular lead. Remember, you may double inferentially in such cases.)

36

In addition, you may double certain bids to direct a lead or allow partner to compete with length in the suit. These include:

1. A Stayman response of 2 ♣. Avoid this, however, unless your clubs are as good as K-J-10-x-x. Opener may redouble with four or more clubs.
2. Blackwood and Gerber responses. Partner is entitled to take inference if you do *not* double.
3. Transfer responses.
4. Bids of the *fourth suit*, which often suggest a partial stopper or A-x-x and suggest that partner bid notrump if possible.

| South | West | North | East |
|-------|------|-------|------|
|       | 1 ♠  | Pass  | 2 ♢  |
| Pass  | 2 ♡  | Pass  | 3 ♣  |
| ?     |      |       |      |

You, South, hold:        ♠ 5 4
                           ♡ A 7 6
                           ♢ 7 6 5
                           ♣ K Q 10 7 5

Double. If you do not, and West now bids 3 NT, partner will probably get off to the wrong lead.

## IV. DOUBLES THAT SHOW GENERAL STRENGTH

If the opponents climb into your auction with a conventional bid, your first move may be to *double,* telling partner that your side has most of the high-card strength. From then on, either one of you may elect to double for penalty or bid game.

| South | West | North | East |
|-------|------|-------|------|
|       |      | 1 ♠   | 2 NT |
| ?     |      |       |      |

East's action is the Unusual Notrump, showing length in both minor suits. You, South, hold:

$$\spadesuit \ Q \ 4$$
$$\heartsuit \ A \ J \ 7 \ 3 \ 2$$
$$\diamondsuit \ K \ 6$$
$$\clubsuit \ J \ 8 \ 6 \ 5$$

Double. If the opponents run to diamonds, partner may be able to double them. If they bail out to clubs, you may double if the vulnerability permits. Otherwise you will bid hearts or notrump.

## V. THE REDOUBLE

In the hands of a knowledgeable player, the redouble can be a flexible, effective tool. But no other call is so underrated and misused.

1. To take the obvious first, a redouble is available if you want to re-express your confidence in making your bid. Sometimes it can be hard to resist the temptation to try for a glorious victory by redoubling viciously when doubled. The fact is, though, that the opponents usually know something you don't when they dare to double a player of your caliber. Don't redouble unless *you* know something *they* don't.

Partner opened 1 ♡ and went to 4 ♡ after you raised. Your RHO doubles.

(a)    ♠ K Q x          (b)    ♠ A 10 x x
       ♡ x x x                      ♡ Q 9 x x
       ◇ Q J x x x                ◇ x
       ♣ J x                       ♣ J 10 x x

(a)   Pass despite your maximum point count. The opponents' top cards will cash, and you can do nothing about the likely trump stack. Running to 4 NT might even be the winning action!

(b)   You may redouble, especially if in need of points. (If you're like me, that means you would *always* redouble.) You have *four* nice hearts, so the enemy is less likely to take a lot of trump tricks (always your chief worry); your controls are good as well, so some of their high-card strength may not be as productive as they hope.

2. The redouble when partner's opening bid is doubled for takeout is familiar. Traditionally, responder is supposed to redouble with 10 high-card points or more, informing opener that the hand belongs to them. The opponents will not be allowed to declare undoubled.

Partner opened 1♡, RHO doubled.

(a) ♠ K J 9 x
    ♡ Q x
    ◇ Q 10 x x x
    ♣ A x

(b) ♠ x x
    ♡ K Q x
    ◇ A x x x
    ♣ J x x x

(c) ♠ x x
    ♡ K Q x x
    ◇ A J x x
    ♣ K x x

(d) ♠ K Q 10 x x x
    ♡ A x
    ◇ x x
    ♣ K x x

A redouble is the correct action on all four of these hands.

(a) If the opponents run to spades or diamonds, you can double. If they try clubs, perhaps your redouble will allow your partner to double *that*. (Note, however, that the vulnerability is always a factor in judging whether to double the opponents or bid on. This is particularly true at matchpoint scoring.)
(b) Support hearts at the minimum level at your next turn.
(c) Support hearts with a jump next.
(d) Bid spades (forcing) next.

3. Even if you have 10 high-card points, a redouble isn't always your best action over a takeout double. If you have an offensive hand with several features to show, spending a round of bidding to redouble may be shortsighted. You may do better to start describing your hand.

Partner opened 1♣, RHO doubled.

(a) ♠ x x
    ♡ A Q 10 x x
    ◇ x x
    ♣ K J x x

(b) ♠ x
    ♡ A Q x x x
    ◇ K J x x x
    ♣ x x

(c)　♠ x
　　 ♡ A x x
　　 ◇ K 10 x x
　　 ♣ Q J x x x

(d)　♠ K
　　 ♡ K
　　 ◇ Q J x x x
　　 ♣ Q 10 x x x x

(a)　You want to show a fair hand with a heart suit and a club fit. If you redouble, it may go 1 ♠ on your left, 2 ♠ on your right. Now you wouldn't have room to show all your features below the four level, where you would risk a possible minus. Just bid 1 ♡ over the double and plan to support clubs next.

(b)　Same idea. Competition may crowd the auction, so start bidding your suits. Respond 1 ♡.

(c)　You prefer to get in a club raise immediately, rather than redouble and give the opponents a chance to get together in spades. A convention such as *Jordan* (in which a 2 NT response shows a limit raise in opener's suit) is helpful here.

(d)　This hand is from Terence Reese's book *Develop Your Bidding Judgment*. Reese likes a 4 ♣ bid over the double. At least one of the major-suit kings will be worthless for offense, and the opponents could have a big fit in one of the majors. Preemption looks more realistic than a redouble.

4. How about SOS redoubles? These are useful in pair events, where making any *doubled* contract is always worth a fine score, and *business* redoubles are a case of overkill.

You open 1 ♣, LHO doubled, partner and RHO passed.

♠ A J x
♡ Q 10 x x
◇ K x x
♣ A x x

Redouble. The opponents say they have you nailed in 1 ♣ doubled, and you have no reason to disagree. Partner should pick another suit.

You open 1 ♣, LHO and partner pass, RHO reopens with a double.

(a)    ♠ A J x              (b)    ♠ x
       ♡ Q 10 x x                 ♡ x x
       ◊ K x x                      ◊ Q J x
       ♣ A x x                      ♣ A K Q 10 x x x

(c)    ♠ A Q x
       ♡ A x x
       ◊ x x
       ♣ A K Q 10 x

(a)    Pass. Don't scream before you are hurt. If LHO passes for penalty, partner is still there and can start rescue operations.
(b)    You preempt, of course. Knowing that the opponents almost surely have a game, you bid as many clubs as the vulnerability allows.
(c)    Redouble. Obviously, this is *not* for rescue. You are just telling partner not to give up yet. The deal may belong to your side even though partner couldn't respond to 1 ♣.

There are other occasions when a redouble shows general strength . . .

For example:

5. You open 1 ♣, partner responds 1 ♡, RHO doubles.

(a)    ♠ A x x             (b)    ♠ x
       ♡ A x                    ♡ K Q x x
       ◊ J x x                    ◊ x x
       ♣ A K Q 10 x            ♣ A K Q x x x

(a)    Redouble. This doesn't necessarily promise a fit for partner's suit. It just advises him that your side has most of the high-card strength. Depending on your holdings, you may proceed to double the opponents or bid further.
(b)    Do not redouble. Jump to 3 ♡ or 4 ♡.

Partner opens 1♡, and you raise to 2♡. This is passed around to your RHO, who reopens with a double.

(c)  ♠ A Q 10 x    (d)  ♠ x
     ♡ 10 x x           ♡ Q x x x
     ◊ J 10 x x         ◊ A x x
     ♣ Q x              ♣ x x x x x

(c)  Redouble in a flash. You could hardly have a better hand for your single raise. You can safely double if the opponents run to 2♠ or 3◊. (Partner, who knows you have a heart fit, can always pull with an unsuitable hand.) If they bid clubs, perhaps partner can double.

(d)  Reraise to 3♡ immediately, hoping to shut out the spades.

6. If you and partner are bidding toward slam, and the opponents double a cuebid to direct a lead, you have an extra option that may be useful.

You open 1♡ and partner responds 3♡ (forcing as you play). You cuebid spades, he replies 4♣, and RHO doubles.

(a)  ♠ A K x x    (b)  ♠ A K x x
     ♡ A K J x x        ♡ A K J x x
     ◊ J x x            ◊ J x
     ♣ x                ♣ x x

(a)  Redouble, showing *second-round* control of clubs.
(b)  Pass, *denying* second-round control.

There are other possible schemes. Expert Eddie Kantar recommends that *redouble* here shows *first*-round control, *any bid* promises *second*-round control, and *pass denies* a control. This style would be useful if your partnership cuebids controls *up-the-line* regardless of whether they are first- or second-round.

42

Partner opens 1♡, and you respond 3♡ (forcing). He cuebids 4♣, you answer 4◇. This is doubled on your left and passed back to you.

♠ x x
♡ K Q x x
◇ A K x
♣ Q x x x

Redouble, showing first- *and second* round control in diamonds. (Don't try this with somebody you don't trust; you might end up down 1600 in 4◇ redoubled!)

7. Suppose you open 1 NT, and partner's Stayman response is doubled. When should you consider a redouble?

(a) ♠ A x
    ♡ K 10 x
    ◇ A J x x
    ♣ K J 9 x

(b) ♠ A J x
    ♡ K x x
    ◇ A J 9 x
    ♣ K x x

(c) ♠ A x x
    ♡ K J x
    ◇ A K x x x
    ♣ J x

(d) ♠ A J x x
    ♡ K x
    ◇ A K x x
    ♣ J x x

(a) This is the time to redouble. You suggest four (or more) clubs, usually with two honors, and invite partner to pass. You would redouble on this hand even if one of your diamonds were a heart. You could still get to a major if partner couldn't stand 2♣ redoubled. The same requirements for a redouble apply after doubles of 2◇ (two-way Stayman) and transfer bids.

(b) Pass. This denies a four-card major and *promises a stopper* in clubs.

(c) Bid 2◇. You *deny* a club stopper as well as a four-card major. This way, you can avoid notrump if partner also lacks a club stopper.

(d) Bid 2♣ as usual.

8. We can end up where we started, with two redoubles that aim to score more points.

♠ K 10 x
♡ A J x
◊ A K Q x x x x
♣ —

Partner opens 1♣. You jump to 2◊ and bid 6◊ over partner's 2 NT rebid. RHO doubles.

This is a Lightner double, asking for an unusual lead, usually the lead of dummy's first-bid suit. RHO probably has the ♣AK or ♣AQ, since he is unlikely to be void when you are. If partner's clubs are mediocre, he must have cards in the majors. You should redouble and expect to make at least six.

♠ x
♡ A K Q x x
◊ A x x
♣ K J x x

At matchpoint duplicate, only your side is vulnerable. Partner opens 1◊, you respond 1♡, he raises to 2♡. Suppose you try Blackwood, and partner responds 5♡, two aces. RHO doubles.

Now, don't lose your poise. Your RHO knows (from partner's two-ace reply to 4 NT) that you can make a slam. He's trying to victimize you with the good old *striped-tail ape double*. Whatever you do, don't pass. You will make six or seven, scoring 1050 or 1250, but lose to all the 1430's, 1460's and 2210's. Redoubling will work if there are only 12 tricks (1600 for 5♡ redoubled making six, 1430 for the small slam), but if a grand slam is cold, you will lose points even if you redouble (2000 for 5♡ redoubled making seven, 2210 for the grand). If you redouble, your RHO plans to turn tail like the shy striped-tail ape and run to 5♠. Then you can go ahead and bid your small slam or try for a grand.

# SUMMARY

The DOUBLE is useful in a variety of situations. A double increases the points for defeating an unsuccessful contract, but it also may urge partner to take action. Penalty doubles require good judgment — possession of lots of high-card points, for example, is often not enough to attempt a penalty double.

Some penalty doubles are intended not to earn a bigger penalty but to offer a better chance to defeat the contract — they conventionally request a specific lead. Other doubles inform partner about general strength.

The REDOUBLE is another useful action with many possible applications.

## TEST YOUR COMPREHENSION OF THE MATERIAL IN THIS CHAPTER:

I.   Decide whether you would double the contract in the following situations.

|    | South | West | North | East |  |
|----|-------|------|-------|------|--|
| 1. |       |      |       | 1 NT | ♠ K J 4 3 |
|    | Pass  | 3 NT | Pass  | Pass | ♡ A J 6 |
|    | ?     |      |       |      | ◇ 9 8 |
|    |       |      |       |      | ♣ A K 6 5 |
| 2. |       |      |       | 1 NT | ♠ K Q J 10 4 |
|    | Pass  | 2 NT | Pass  | 3 NT | ♡ J 9 5 4 |
|    | ?     |      |       |      | ◇ A 3 |
|    |       |      |       |      | ♣ 8 7 |
| 3. |       |      |       | 1 ♡  | ♠ J 10 9 7 |
|    | Pass  | 2 ♡  | Pass  | 3 ♡  | ♡ Q J 10 8 |
|    | Pass  | 4 ♡  | Pass  | Pass | ◇ 7 6 |
|    | ?     |      |       |      | ♣ 7 6 5 |
| 4. |       |      |       | 1 ♡  | ♠ 4 3 2 |
|    | Pass  | 1 NT | Pass  | 2 ♠  | ♡ K J 10 4 3 |
|    | Pass  | 3 ♠  | Pass  | 4 ♡  | ◇ J 7 6 |
|    | ?     |      |       |      | ♣ K 6 |

5.

| | | | 1♡ | ♠ 5 |
|---|---|---|---|---|
| Pass | 1♠ | Pass | 1 NT | ♡ K J 9 8 |
| Pass | 2 NT | Pass | 3 NT | ◇ A 9 7 5 |
| ? | | | | ♣ J 10 9 7 |

6.

| | | | 1◇ | ♠ 7 6 5 3 |
|---|---|---|---|---|
| Pass | 3♣ | Pass | 3◇ | ♡ A K 5 |
| Pass | 4♣ | Pass | 4 NT | ◇ J 7 6 |
| Pass | 5♡ | Pass | 6 NT | ♣ 7 6 4 |
| ? | | | | |

7.

| | | 1♠ | 2◇ | ♠ 7 6 |
|---|---|---|---|---|
| ? | | | | ♡ J 7 |
| | | | | ◇ K J 10 6 5 4 |
| | | | | ♣ 8 7 5 |

8.

| | | | 1♡ | ♠ J 9 7 6 |
|---|---|---|---|---|
| Pass | 2♣ | Pass | 3♣ | ♡ A |
| Pass | 3♡ | Pass | 4♡ | ◇ 8 7 6 5 |
| ? | | | | ♣ A 7 6 4 |

II. In each sequence, give the meaning of the double.

| | *South* | *West* | *North* | *East* |
|---|---|---|---|---|
| 1. | 1♠ | 2♣ | 2♠ | Pass |
| | Pass | *Double* | | |

| | | | | |
|---|---|---|---|---|
| 2. | 1◇ | 1♡ | 1 NT | *Double* |

| | | | | |
|---|---|---|---|---|
| 3. | 1♡ | Pass | 2♡ | Pass |
| | Pass | *Double* | | |

| | | | | |
|---|---|---|---|---|
| 4. | 1 NT | Pass | Pass | 2♡ |
| | *Double* | | | |

| | | | | |
|---|---|---|---|---|
| 5. | 1♡ | Pass | 1 NT | *Double* |

| | | | | |
|---|---|---|---|---|
| 6. | 1♡ | Pass | 1♠ | Pass |
| | 2♡ | *Double* | | |

III. Choose a suit to lead against the following doubled contracts.

|     | South | West | North | East |
|-----|-------|------|-------|------|
| 1.  | 1 ◊ | 1 ♡ | 1 NT | Pass |
|     | 3 NT | Double | (All Pass) | |

♠ Q J 10 5 4
♡ 8
◊ 7 6 5
♣ Q 9 5 3

|     | South | West | North | East |
|-----|-------|------|-------|------|
| 2.  | 1 ◊ | Pass | 1 NT | 2 ♠ |
|     | 3 ◊ | Pass | 3 NT | Pass |
|     | Pass | Double | (All Pass) | |

♠ K J 9 6 4
♡ 8 7
◊ K
♣ A J 8 6 4

|     | South | West | North | East |
|-----|-------|------|-------|------|
| 3.  | 1 ◊ | 1 ♡ | 1 NT | 2 ♣ |
|     | 3 ◊ | Pass | 3 NT | Pass |
|     | Pass | Double | (All Pass) | |

♠ Q 10 6 5
♡ 9 4
◊ 8
♣ K J 6 5 4 2

|     | South | West | North | East |
|-----|-------|------|-------|------|
| 4.  | | | 1 ♣ | Pass |
|     | 1 ♠ | Pass | 1 NT | Pass |
|     | 3 NT | Double | (All Pass) | |

♠ 10 3
♡ Q 10 7 5 3
◊ K 7
♣ 7 6 5 4

|     | South | West | North | East |
|-----|-------|------|-------|------|
| 5.  | 1 ◊ | Pass | 1 ♠ | Pass |
|     | 2 ◊ | Pass | 2 ♡ | Pass |
|     | 2 ♠ | Pass | 2 NT | Pass |
|     | 3 NT | Double | (All Pass) | |

♠ J 9 6 4
♡ A 3
◊ 8 7
♣ J 10 6 4 2

|     | South | West | North | East |
|-----|-------|------|-------|------|
| 6.  | | | 1 NT | Pass |
|     | 3 NT | Double | (All Pass) | |

♠ 7
♡ J 9 7 5 3
◊ K 7 6
♣ 8 7 4 2

|     | South | West | North | East |
|-----|-------|------|-------|------|
| 7.  | | | 1 ♠ | Pass |
|     | 2 ♠ | Pass | 4 ♠ | Pass |
|     | Pass | Double | (All Pass) | |

♠ 7
♡ Q J 10
◊ A 6
♣ J 9 7 6 5 4 3

## TEST YOUR COMPREHENSION OF THE MATERIAL ON REDOUBLES:

1.  North, your partner, opens 1♡; East doubles. What do you call with:

    (a)   ♠ K Q 7 5       (b)   ♠ 8 7
          ♡ 8 7                   ♡ K Q 6 5
          ◇ A J 4 3 2          ◇ A Q 7 6
          ♣ J 8                   ♣ Q 6 5

    (c)   ♠ —               (d)   ♠ 7 6 5
          ♡ Q 10 7 6 5       ♡ A 7 6
          ◇ Q J 8 5 3         ◇ A J 4
          ♣ 8 7 5              ♣ J 8 6 4

2.  You, South, open 1♣. West and North pass, and East reopens with a double. What do you call with:

    (a)   ♠ A 6 4          (b)   ♠ 5
          ♡ A K 7             ♡ 5 4
          ◇ 6 5               ◇ K 7 6
          ♣ A K J 7 3        ♣ A K J 8 7 6 5

3.  You, South, open 1♣. North responds 1♡, and East doubles. What do you call with:

    (a)   ♠ A 7 6          (b)   ♠ 4
          ♡ 7 6              ♡ K Q 7 6
          ◇ A K 7           ◇ 4 3
          ♣ A Q 8 7 6        ♣ A K 7 6 5 3

4.  North, your partner, opens 1♡, and you raise to 2♡. After two passes East reopens with a double. What do you call with:

    (a)   ♠ A Q 10 3      (b)   ♠ 3
          ♡ Q 6 4            ♡ Q 7 6 5
          ◇ J 10 7 5        ◇ 8 7 6
          ♣ 5 4              ♣ A 8 7 5 3

5.  You, South, open 1 ♡; North raises to 2 ♡, and East doubles. What do you call with:

(a)  ♠ 6 5          (b)  ♠ 5
     ♡ A K J 7 5          ♡ A K J 6 5 3
     ◊ A 8 7              ◊ K 7 6 5
     ♣ A J 4              ♣ 6 5

6.  You, South, open 1 ♡, and North raises to 3 ♡ (forcing). You cuebid 3 ♠ and he replies 4 ♣, doubled by East. What do you call with:

(a)  ♠ A K 6 5       (b)  ♠ A K 7 6
     ♡ A K 7 5 3          ♡ A K Q 6 5
     ◊ Q 8 5              ◊ J 7
     ♣ 5                  ♣ 7 6

7.  You, South, open 1 NT. North's 2 ♣ response is doubled by East. What do you call with:

(a)  ♠ A 5           (b)  ♠ A 7 5
     ♡ K 10 4             ♡ K J 5
     ◊ A J 7 5            ◊ A K 6 5 3
     ♣ K J 9 4            ♣ J 7

(c)  ♠ A J 7          (d)  ♠ A J 7 5
     ♡ K 10 4             ♡ K 8
     ◊ A K 8 5            ◊ A K 6 5
     ♣ K 8 6              ♣ J 7 5

## SOLUTIONS TO QUIZ ON DOUBLES

I.  1.  No. Dummy will probably have a long diamond suit.
    2.  Yes. You'll probably beat them with a spade lead.
    3.  Yes. Double inferentially.
    4.  No. They may run to spades and make it.
    5.  Yes. Double inferentially.
    6.  No. They may run to 7 ♣ and make it without a heart lead.
    7.  No.
    8.  Yes. Lead the ♣ A and another club. Partner should ruff.

II.  1.  Takeout
     2.  Penalty
     3.  Takeout
     4.  Penalty (when *behind* the 2♡ bidder)
     5.  Takeout (of hearts)
     6.  Penalty
III. 1.  Heart
     2.  Spade. Partner should have a spade card.
     3.  Heart
     4.  Spade. Dummy's first-bid suit.
     5.  Club. Make your normal lead, since dummy *rebid* diamonds.
     6.  Spade. Make an unusual lead.
     7.  Club. Partner is probably void. Lead the *three* as a suit-preference signal for diamonds.

## SOLUTIONS TO QUIZ ON REDOUBLES

I.   1. a.  Redouble
        b.  Redouble
        c.  4♡
        d.  Redouble
     2. a.  Redouble
        b.  3♣ or 4♣, depending on the vulnerability.
     3. a.  Redouble
        b.  3♡
     4. a.  Redouble
        b.  3♡
     5. a.  Redouble
        b.  3♡
     6. a.  Redouble
        b.  Pass
     7. a.  Redouble
        b.  2◊
        c.  Pass
        d.  2♠

# Chapter 4

## INFERENCE AND INFERENTIAL COUNTING

If bridge only amounted to obeying rules, the game would not enjoy such a wide following. The key to enjoying the game and becoming a winner is learning how to *reason* at the table. A bridge game is a series of little problems, some of which cannot be handled by applying rules. An aptitude for solving puzzles in logic or mathematics is an attribute of many good bridge players. You must be able to think for yourself. In this chapter we discuss problem solving at the bridge table.

An *inference* is a conclusion deduced from evidence through analysis. When declarer tries to work out the defenders' high cards and distribution, the ability to draw inferences is useful. Suppose you are declarer in a heart contract. Dummy holds A-Q-10-8-4 of clubs and you have a small singleton. Your right-hand opponent wins the opening lead in another suit and switches to a trump. Where do you think the missing club honors are? Would RHO lead a passive trump if his club holding were x-x-x or J-x-x? No, he would be afraid you would establish the clubs and get discards for your losers. He would try to cash side-suit tricks quickly. To justify his line of defense, your RHO must have good clubs, probably both the king and jack. You have drawn an inference from the opponents' play.

*INFERENCE AND INFERENTIAL COUNTING CAN HELP YOU SOLVE THE MOST PUZZLING MYSTERIES.*

When drawing such inferences, you must take the opponents' skill into consideration. You can draw some simple inferences against beginning players, while others are reliable only if you trust the opponents' defense implicitly. Against top experts, you may be able to draw subtle inferences (which makes the game more fun). In any case, don't base a play on the assumption that your opponent has erred. You'll feel bad if it turns out he was playing correctly all the time.

1.
♠ J 8 6 4 3
♡ A J 4
◊ A Q
♣ J 5 3

♠ K Q 10 7 2
♡ K 10 5
◊ 5 4
♣ Q 9 2

West dealt and opened 1 ♣. You and partner then bid to 4 ♠. West leads the ♣A, ♣K and another club. Luckily for you, East follows to all three rounds, and you win the third trick. You lead the ♠K, and West wins the ace as East shows out. You finesse the queen successfully on the diamond return and draw the rest of the trumps. Both opponents follow low when you cash the ◊ A. Now you must guess the ♡Q. **Do you have an inspiration?**

Let's see what we know about West's hand. He had three spades to the ace and three or four clubs to the A-K. That's six or seven cards in the black suits, so he had six or seven red cards. **How do you think his red cards are divided?** West opened the bidding in a suit of at most four cards, so he can't have five diamonds or five hearts — he would have opened in that suit. West's red cards should be divided 3-3, 4-3 or 4-2. The point is that West seems to have had a fairly *balanced* hand.

**How many high-card points has West shown?** ♣A, ♣K, ♠A, ◊ K. That's 14, right? Suppose West had the ♡Q as well. He would have a balanced hand with 16 high-card points. What would the opening bid have been? Right, 1 NT. So you should play *East* for the ♡Q.

2.   ♠ K 4
   ♡ J 5 3
   ◊ J 4 2
   ♣ K J 7 5 2

   ♠ 8 5
   ♡ K Q 10 9 6 4
   ◊ A
   ♣ A 10 8 3

East opened 1 ♠, you overcalled and got to 4 ♡. The opening lead is a spade, and East cashes the queen and ace. He then plays the trump ace and another trump, and you win as West follows. Both opponents play low on a club to the king, and East follows with the nine when you lead a club back from dummy. You should play the *ace*, expecting the queen to drop. West would almost certainly have *led* a singleton club against this contract. In fact, the opponents could always defeat 4 ♡ if West had only one club. Note that East could have opened with the ♠A, ♠Q, ♡A and ◊K. Counting points is inconclusive. Instead, you infer from the *way the opponents defend.*

3.   ♠ A 5 3
   ♡ 7 5 3
   ◊ A 7 4
   ♣ K 7 5 3

   ♠ K J 8 6 2
   ♡ J 9
   ◊ K J 5
   ♣ 10 8 2

West opened 1 ♡, passed around to you. You balanced with 1 ♠, North raised to 2 ♠, and all passed. West leads the ◊ 10, East plays the queen, and you win. **How should you play the trumps?** West's failure to lead a heart marks East with a heart honor. (West would surely lead a heart in preference to a diamond if he held A-K or K-Q.) If East has a high heart as well as the ◊ Q, he cannot have the ♠Q. He would have responded to the opening bid. So you should play for the drop of the ♠Q.

53

4.
 ♠ 8 5
 ♡ K 9 8 3
 ◇ K 5
 ♣ K Q J 8 5

 ♠ A K Q 6 4
 ♡ A J 10 4
 ◇ A 7
 ♣ 9 2

The auction, with the opponents silent, was:
| 1♠ | 2♣ |
|----|----|
| 2♡ | 4♡ |
| 6♡ |    |

West leads the ♣A and switches to the ◇J. **How should you play the trumps?** All other things being equal, you should play West for the queen. Cashing the ace of dummy's bid suit (instead of leading the unbid suit) would be a doubtful play unless your opponent expected to beat the contract with a trump trick if he snatched the ♣A.

5.
 ♠ A Q 6
 ♡ 6 5 3 2
 ◇ K 7 4
 ♣ 8 4 2

 ♠ K 5 2
 ♡ A K 4
 ◇ Q 9
 ♣ Q J 9 7 5

The contract is 2 NT, and the opening lead is the ◇5, riding to the queen. You play a spade to the queen and a club to your jack and West's king. West now plays the ◇A and ◇2. Dummy wins, and East follows to both rounds. East plays low when you lead another club from dummy. You should *finesse the ♣9*. West indicated a sure entry to his diamond winners by clearing the suit. Had he been entryless, he would have led a second low diamond, keeping communication with his partner's hand.

6.
          ♠ A K 8 4
          ♡ 7 4
          ◇ 8 5 3
          ♣ 7 5 4 2

          ♠ 2
          ♡ K Q J 10 9 3
          ◇ A Q 2
          ♣ A Q 6

Against your 4 ♡ contract, the opening lead is the ♠ Q. You play the ace and king, discarding a diamond, and finesse the ◇ Q to West's king. A spade forces you to ruff. Now the ♡ K is won by East, who returns a club! If you respect East's defense at all, you should expect West to have the ♣ K. If the club finesse were going to work, East would never give you an opportunity to take it when he could exit safely in some other suit. Play West for the singleton or doubleton ♣ K.

7.
          ♠ Q
          ♡ K 9 6 4
          ◇ A 10 7 4
          ♣ K 8 6 4

          ♠ 10
          ♡ A Q J 10 5
          ◇ K Q 8 6 2
          ♣ A 7

You bid to a good 6 ♡ with no interference. The opening lead is the ♠ A, followed by a trump switch. You draw the rest of the trumps and only need to pick up the diamonds without loss. If *East* had a void in diamonds, he might have doubled 6 ♡, suggesting an unusual lead. So if anyone is void, it should be West. You should play a diamond to the ace.

*Counting the distribution* of the opponents' hands can help indicate your best line of play or suggest where a crucial card is hiding. It is usually possible to get a count as the play proceeds. When you need a distributional count early in the play, however (possibly because you face a guess in *trumps*), you may have to *infer* the distribution of the concealed hands based on the bidding and the early play. Here is an example:

8.
      ♠ A 7 5
      ♡ 9 7 5
      ◇ Q 9 6 5
      ♣ K 6 4

      ♠ K 2
      ♡ A 4 3
      ◇ 10 4 2
      ♣ A J 10 5 3

| *South* | *West* | *North* | *East* |
|---------|--------|---------|--------|
|         | 1 ◇    | Pass    | 1 ♡    |
| 2 ♣     | 2 ♡    | 3 ♣     | (All Pass) |

West leads the ◇ AK and another diamond. East follows once and ruffs the third round low. You win the heart shift. If you can draw all the trumps, you can discard one of your heart losers on the ◇ Q and make the contract, losing only one more trick. But if you misguess in trumps, you will go down at least one. **What is your plan?**

Let's try to infer the distribution.

| | |
|---|---|
| DIAMONDS are known to be 5-1. | No inference necessary. |
| HEARTS must be . . . . . . . . . 3-4. | East needed a four-card suit to bid hearts, but West needed at least three-card support to raise. |
| SPADES must be . . . . . . . . . . 4-4. | If either opponent had five spades, the suit would have been bid. West would open 1 ♠ with five spades and five diamonds; East would respond 1 ♠ with five spades and four hearts. |
| *so* CLUBS must be . . . . . . . . . . . 1-4. | Play the ♣K and finesse through East. |

56

9.
    ♠ 4 3
    ♡ A 7 5 3
    ◇ K 10 7 5
    ♣ Q 10 5

    ♠ A Q J 2
    ♡ 4 2
    ◇ A J 9 6
    ♣ 8 6 2

| South | West | North | East |
|-------|------|-------|------|
|  |  |  | 1 ♣ |
| Pass | 1 ♠ | Pass | 2 ♠ |
| Pass | Pass | Double | Pass |
| 3 ◇ | (All Pass) |  |  |

Partner's balancing double asked you to choose one of the unbid suits. Since your diamonds were strong, you bid when you could have gambled a pass. The opening lead is the ♣J. East wins dummy's queen with the king, cashes the ace, West following, and leads a third club, which West ruffs low. A spade now goes to the king and your ace. **How do you play the trumps?**

CLUBS are known to be . . . 2-5.

SPADES must be . . . . . . . . 4-3.   West needed four cards to bid the suit, but East had to have at least three to raise.

HEARTS should be . . . . . . . 3-4.   If West had four hearts, he would respond *1♡* to the opening bid, bidding his suits *up-the-line*. But East would have opened 1♡ with five clubs and five hearts.

*so* DIAMONDS are . . . . . . . . . 4-1.   Cash the ◇A and lead low to the ten.

10.                     ♠ K 10 7 3
                        ♡ 10 9 8 5
                        ◇ J 6
                        ♣ A Q 4

                        ♠ J 8 4
                        ♡ —
                        ◇ A K 9 8 7 4 2
                        ♣ 10 9 8

This hand is taken from Marshall Miles' excellent book, *All 52 Cards*. East opened 1 ♣, you overcalled 3 ◇, and West doubled. The opening lead is the ♣2, East winning the king when you played low from dummy. You ruff the heart return. Should you play safe in trumps by leading toward the jack (necessary if West has all four of the missing diamonds) or play trumps from the top?

Miles points out that East should probably have no more than four clubs. If he were void in diamonds, he would have five cards in a major suit and would have opened in his major. So the correct play is to lay down a top diamond. As it happens, West has ◇ Q10x and a small doubleton spade. You go down on a spade ruff if you lead toward the ◇ J.

The subject of drawing inferences from the opponents' bidding and play is broad, and we have examined only a few times when inferences are available. A trump opening lead can be significant, to mention another common situation. Suppose they lead a trump after this bidding:

1 ♠          1 NT
2 ♡          Pass

Your opponent thinks you will need to ruff spades in dummy. He may have good spades or he may have very few and think his partner has a good spade holding.

A trump lead after an auction like:

1 ♡          2 ♣
2 ♡          4 ♡

suggests that your opponent thinks dummy's club suit will not be a good source of tricks. He may have good clubs or very few. If he had x-x-x or, particularly, Q-x-x or K-x-x, he would make an attacking lead, fearing that the clubs would provide discards.

After

1 ♡         3 ♡
4 ♡


a trump lead suggests that your opponent has honors in the other suits and wants to avoid leading from them. He chose a trump lead for safety.

---

## SUMMARY

An *INFERENCE* is an assumption deduced from evidence. The ability to draw inferences from the bidding, the opening lead and the defenders' later strategy can be helpful.

A *count of the opponents' distribution* can indicate a good line of play or help locate a vital missing card. Usually, a count becomes available as the play proceeds and the defenders discard. When you need a count early in the play, however, you may be able to get one *inferentially,* using clues from the bidding and the early play.

Success at drawing inferences depends on the strength of your opponents. If you can trust them to bid and play logically, many delicate inferences are available.

## TEST YOUR COMPREHENSION OF THE MATERIAL IN THIS CHAPTER:

1.
&spades; A Q 4 3
&hearts; K 4 3
&diams; 8 6
&clubs; A 9 6 4

&spades; K J 9 6 2
&hearts; 7 5
&diams; A 7
&clubs; K Q 10 2

You open 1 &spades; and arrive at 4 &spades; without interference. The opening lead is the &diams; J. You win, draw trumps and exit with a diamond. West wins and leads the &hearts; J. The king is covered by East's ace, and you ruff the third heart. All follow low to the &clubs; K. What is your next play?

2.
&spades; 10 4 3
&hearts; A 9 4 3
&diams; Q 10 5
&clubs; K 10 3

&spades; A 7
&hearts; Q J 10 8 6 5
&diams; 8 6 3
&clubs; Q 6

| South | West | North | East |
|-------|------|-------|------|
|       |      |       | Pass |
| Pass  | 1 &diams; | Pass | 2 &clubs; |
| 2 &hearts; | 3 &clubs; | 3 &hearts; | (All Pass) |

West leads the &diams; A, &diams; K and another diamond. East follows twice and ruffs the third round low. You win the spade return. When you lead the &hearts; Q, West plays low. Can you get out of this for down just one?

3.               ♠ K 4 3 2
               ♡ J 4 3 2
               ♢ 3 2
               ♣ K 3 2

               ♠ Q 8 7 6 5
               ♡ K
               ♢ A J 10
               ♣ A Q J 4

You open 1 ♠ *after three passes* and wind up in 4 ♠. West leads the ♢ K, and you win. What is your next play?

4.               ♠ Q 10 7 5 3
               ♡ 3 2
               ♢ K 5
               ♣ Q 10 6 5

               ♠ A K J 9 2
               ♡ K J
               ♢ 7 2
               ♣ A J 9 4

You open 1 ♠ *after three passes* and end in 4 ♠. West leads the ♢ J. East wins the ♢ A and ♢ Q and shifts to a low heart. Do you play the king or the jack?

5.               ♠ J 8
               ♡ K 10 3 2
               ♢ Q 7 6 5
               ♣ 7 6 5

               ♠ A 9
               ♡ A Q 4
               ♢ A K J 9
               ♣ K 4 3 2

You open 2 NT, and partner raises you to 3 NT. LHO leads the ♠ 2. Dummy's jack is covered by the queen, and you win. You cash four rounds of diamonds, RHO following and LHO following once

and discarding a spade and two clubs. Both opponents follow to the
♡ A and ♡ Q, and LHO plays the nine when you lead a third heart
toward dummy. What do you do?

6.                        ♠ K 10 3 2
                         ♡ 9 7 5
                         ◇ Q 10 4
                         ♣ J 7 6

                         ♠ A J 9 5 4
                         ♡ A K Q 2
                         ◇ J 9 8
                         ♣ 3

You open 1♠ after three passes, partner raises to 2♠, you go
on to 4♠. LHO leads a low club. RHO wins the ♣K and tries to
cash the ace, which you ruff. How should you play trumps?

7.                        ♠ 5 4 3
                         ♡ A K 5 4
                         ◇ K J 10 7 6 5
                         ♣ —

                         ♠ A K Q 2
                         ♡ Q 10 7 6 3 2
                         ◇ A 8 2
                         ♣ —

Partner opens 1◇, you respond 1♡; he raises to 2♡, you try
5 NT, the *Grand Slam Force*. He puts you in 7♡. The opening lead
is a trump(!) You win and draw another round, LHO showing out.
You play four rounds of spades, ruffing the last one in dummy. LHO
follows twice and then discards two clubs, RHO follows to all four
spades. How do you play diamonds?

# SOLUTIONS

1. Play the ♣Q next. If *West* had a singleton club, he might have led it, especially since he seems to have had a poor hand.

2. West had five diamonds (known), at least three clubs (since he raised that suit) and *four spades*. If either East or West had held five spades, the suit would have been bid. So West cannot have another heart. Play the *ace* from dummy, dropping East's king.

3. You want to lead the first round of trumps *through* the defender with the ace, saving a trick if the ace is a singleton. Your first play should be the ♡K. If West has the ♡A as well as the ◇K and ◇Q, he cannot have the ace of trumps. (He would have opened the bidding.) You will know to make the first trump lead *from dummy*. (The lead of the ♡K is a *discovery* play.)

4. You must assume that East has the ♣K, and your eventual club finesse will work. So you cannot play East for the ♡A. You would be (hypothetically) giving him an opening bid. Play the ♡J, hoping East has a hand like:

   ♠ x
   ♡ Q x x x
   ◇ A Q x x
   ♣ K x x x

   This is an example of what Terence Reese called a *second-degree assumption* — first you assume that a certain card lies favorably; then you see how your assumption affects the location of other cards.

5. West had four spades and one diamond. His hearts and clubs must be divided 4-4. With a five-card suit he would have led that suit against 3 NT. So you should play the ♡10 from dummy.

6. East has the ♣A and ♣K, and must have one of the diamond honors (since West would have led a diamond with both honors). So West should have the ♠Q. If East had it, he would have opened the bidding. Play the ♠A and continue with a spade to the *ten*.

7. West had two spades and one heart, and he should have no more than seven clubs. Surely he would have been in the auction with an *eight*-card club suit. So West should have at least three diamonds. Play the ◇A and finesse the ◇J.

# Chapter 5

## IMPROVING YOUR VISUALIZATION

The classical approach to bidding has been that you and partner conduct a dialogue, a conversation between equals. You describe your hand to partner, he does the same for you. Eventually, one of you makes a bid that describes his hand and narrowly defines his strength. At this point the other player becomes the *captain* of the partnership. It is up to him, now that he knows the combined assets of the partnership, to suggest a contract.

A bidding dialogue may be long and scientific, or it may be cut short by a player who is willing to bash into what he thinks is a good spot. But everyone agrees that early, probing bids should be as descriptive as possible. For example, suppose you deal and hold:

> ♠ A 10 x
> ♡ A x x
> ◇ A K J x
> ♣ x x x

You open 1 NT, partner responds 2 ♣; you rebid 2 ◇, partner tries 2 ♠. By agreement, partner's sequence is *invitational* to game. **What should your next action be?**

You should certainly offer encouragement with your top cards and spade fit. Your best bid is 3 ◇, showing where most of your side strength lies. (This bid cannot suggest diamonds as trumps; without spade support you would return to notrump even with a diamond suit.) Partner can now bid **4♠** with:

> ♠ K Q x x x
> ♡ x x x x
> ◇ Q x x
> ♣ x

With this hand:

♠ K Q x x x
♡ x x x x
◇ x
♣ Q x x

he will return to just *3♠*.

As a rule, you and partner try to exchange as much information as you can before placing the contract. Unless you are fairly sure of the place to play, you avoid making an irrevocable decision. Make a further effort to describe your hand instead.

Suppose you hold:

♠ A 10 3
♡ K J 5 4 2
◇ Q 6 4
♣ K 6

| You | Partner |
|-----|---------|
| 1 ♡ | 2 ◇ |
| 2 NT | 3 ♣ |
| 3 ◇ | 3 ♡ |
| ? | |

**What should you bid now?**

Bid *3 ♠*. This is a flexible action that will give your partner useful information. He can almost hear you speaking: "Partner, I have something good in spades, but my holding is not so strong that I want to insist on notrump. My hearts are not so good that I'm anxious to play 4 ♡ opposite x-x-x or a doubleton honor. Nor am I willing to bid four of a minor and take us past 3 NT. I'm leaving it up to you. Bid 3 NT with a little help in spades; 4 ♡ if your support is better than I could expect; or, if you wish, four of a minor."

Your partner should be able to *visualize* your hand very accurately after this descriptive sequence — and finally we have come to the theme of this chapter, VISUALIZATION. In every auction, someone must take the bull by the horns and make the decisive bid. Once your partner's bidding has given you every bit of information, you may still have to conjure up an *image of his high cards and distribu-*

*YOUR VISUALIZATION WILL BECOME CLEARER
WITH CONCENTRATION AND PRACTICE.*

---

*tion,* decide how well it will complement your own, and judge your prospects in the play. Forming a picture of your partner's hand from his bidding (and from the opponents' bidding as well) is an important skill.

Many players think only of their own cards, but good players look further. They mentally place certain cards around the table during the auction and estimate how good the chances will be in the contract they are considering. One rule of thumb good players use is this:

---

IF A SUITABLE MINIMUM FOR PARTNER'S BIDDING
WILL MAKE THE CONTRACT LAYDOWN, BID IT.

---

For example, if you hold:

♠ A K 8 5 4 3
♡ A J 7 6
◇ K 3
♣ 3

66

and partner raises your 1 ♠ opening to 2 ♠ , you can count your points if you want to; but a realistic approach is to make yourself a heavy favorite in 4 ♠ if partner has no more than the ♡K and ♠J-x-x-x. Therefore, you can hardly do less than bid game.

The important corollary to this rule of thumb is:

> IF YOU ARE CONSIDERING A CONTRACT FOR WHICH PARTNER MUST HOLD JUST THE RIGHT CARDS, FORGET IT.

Such specific optimism seldom pays. If you play your partner for certain cards, he won't have them.

You probably visualize your partner's hand more than you realize. If, for instance, a 1 ♡ opening on your left is passed around to you, you balance with 1 NT on:

> ♠ A 10 4
> ♡ J 5 4
> ◇ K 9 6 4
> ♣ K 6 2

True, you don't have a heart stopper. But you know that partner has some points, and maybe a strong hand, since the opponents have stopped low. Since partner failed to act over 1 ♡, he is likely to have heart length and strength. So you bid notrump, visualizing a stopper in his hand.

1.
> ♠ J 4
> ♡ 7 6 4
> ◇ A K J 3
> ♣ A Q 7 5

| South | West | North | East |
|-------|------|-------|------|
|       | 1 ♡  | 1 ♠   | 2 ♡  |
| ?     |      |       |      |

Bid 3 ♡ . You should drive this hand to game. Partner must have either very good spades or a two-suited hand. When you have this much high-card strength, and the opponents are bidding on both sides of you, what is left for partner to hold?

2.

♠ A Q 6 4
♡ 5
♢ A J 4 3
♣ 10 9 7 4

| South | West | North | East |
|-------|------|-------|------|
|       | 1 ♣  | Pass  | 1 ◊  |
| Pass  | 2 ◊  | Double | Pass |
| ?     |      |       |      |

Partner's double is for *takeout*. **Do you like your chances in spades?** You should be able to take at least ten tricks! Are you worried about all those minor-suit losers? Think about it. Partner is marked with a singleton diamond on this bidding. He also has a decent hand with five hearts (the opponents presumably do not have an eight-card heart fit), yet he failed to overcall 1 ♡ at his first turn. Partner must have *bad hearts* to explain that. So where *are* his values? Not in diamonds. He must have good *clubs* (and spades), so you should get some help for your club losers.

3. Both sides vulnerable.

♠ 7 6 5 3
♡ A 9 5 3
♢ A Q 10 4
♣ 5

| South | West | North | East |
|-------|------|-------|------|
|       |      |       | 1 ♠  |
| Pass  | 2 ♠  | 3 ♡   | 3 ♠  |
| ?     |      |       |      |

**How do you like your hand?** Partner should have a *good heart suit* to enter at the three level, vulnerable, between two bidding opponents. He has one spade at most and may have none. Any diamond finesse, taken through the opening bidder, figures to work. Partner should have decent high-card strength, possibly including the ♣ A. Give him this suitable minimum:

♠ —
♡ K Q 10 6 4 2
◊ J 9 3
♣ A 8 7 4

and he might well take 13 tricks! It would be conservative to bid less than 6♡ at this point, but few players would bid more than game. They don't visualize.

In an international match a few years ago, two outstanding players missed a slam with these cards:

4. *Opener*

♠ A 5
♡ 6
◊ K 4
♣ K Q 10 8 6 5 4 2

*Responder*

♠ K Q 7 4 2
♡ A 10 4
◊ 8 7 5
♣ A 7

| | |
|---|---|
| 1♣ | 1♠ |
| 3♣ | 3♡ |
| 5♣ | Pass |

Responder must have been worried about diamond losers when he passed 5♣. However, opener was marked with something good in diamonds. How could he jump to an 11-trick contract without the ♣A, ♡A and some spade honors if he was looking at two or three low diamonds as well?

5. Both sides vulnerable.

♠ J 6 3
♡ A K 8 6 4
◊ 7 6
♣ K 6 5

| South | West | North | East |
|---|---|---|---|
| | | 1◊ | Pass |
| 1♡ | 1♠ | Pass | Pass |
| ? | | | |

69

**What is partner's hand like?** He does not have four hearts (and most players, afraid of losing a heart fit, would raise on *three*-card support here); he is unlikely to have six diamonds or a diamond-club two-suiter. He probably has a balanced minimum. About three-fourths of the time, he will have something in spades, maybe even four cards. Your best call is double. If partner has what you expect, West will go down two or three. Partner is free to pull your double, since you do not promise a stack in spades when you double *in front of* overcaller's suit. If partner leaves your double in, you can expect him to lead a heart, which will be a good start for the defense.

We have seen that visualization and hand evaluation are tied together. Here is a good illustration:

6. Partner opened 2 NT, you responded 3 ♣, and he replied 3 ◇.
   **Which of these two hands would you rather hold to bid a slam?**

(a)  ♠ K J 3       (b)  ♠ K 8 3
     ♡ Q J 5 4           ♡ Q J 5 4
     ◇ 7 6 5             ◇ 7 6 5
     ♣ A 7 6             ♣ A J 6

You should prefer hand (b). Having denied four spades, partner is likely to have A-Q or A-Q-x, in which case your ♠J is worthless. But the ♣ J in hand (b) could be a useful card.

7. North-South vulnerable.
                ♠ J 9 6 5 4 2
                ♡ 5
                ◇ Q 10 4
                ♣ K J 6

| South | West | North | East |
|-------|------|-------|------|
|       |      | 1 ◇   | 1 ♡  |
| 1 ♠   | Pass | 2 ♣   | Pass |
| 2 ◇   | Pass | 3 ♣   | Pass |
| ?     |      |       |      |

Partner is still interested in game even though your bidding warns of weakness. He has at least ten minor-suit cards and should have some heart length, since the opponents failed to compete vigorously in that suit. Partner is likely to be void in spades! That means his high-card values are mainly in the suits he bid. You have just the right hand for partner, with no wasted spade honors opposite his shortness, and minor-suit help. Jump to 5 ◇ and don't be surprised if you make six. (Maybe partner can *bid* six.) Perhaps a 3 ♡ cuebid is an even better action!

8. Neither side vulnerable.

♠ 7 6
♡ 4
◇ A K J 6 5
♣ A Q 10 6 5

| South | West | North | East |
|-------|------|-------|------|
|       | 3 ♠  | 4 ♡   | Double |
| ?     |      |       |      |

**Would you start rescue operations?** (You could bid 4 NT to ask for a choice of the minor suits.) This is somewhat like problem 1. When you have this much high-card strength, and East has doubled, there is nothing left for partner to hold but long, strong hearts. You should hope for the best right where you are. (Note that partner probably has two or three spades, so a minor-suit fit is unlikely.)

9. Neither side vulnerable.

♠ Q 10 8 6
♡ Q 10 5
◇ 10 6 5
♣ J 5 3

| South | West | North | East |
|-------|------|-------|------|
|       |      |       | 1 ◇ |
| Pass  | 1 ♠  | Pass  | 2 ♣ |
| Pass  | Pass | Double | Pass |
| ?     |      |       |      |

Partner must have a fine hand, judging from your weakness and the fact that this is not a safe auction on which to balance. **Why did he not bid at his first turn?** The best explanation is that he has spade length and preferred to trap initially. *2♠* is your best bid. You probably have a fit in that suit and have no guaranteed fit elsewhere.

10. *Partner*    *You*
   1 ◇        1 ♡
   1 NT

**How many diamonds does partner have?** He does not have four hearts or four spades, so he surely has four or more diamonds.

*Partner*    *You*
1 ◇        1 ♠
1 NT

Partner is still likely to have four or more diamonds. He would usually open 1 ♣ with a 3-4-3-3 pattern.

11. **What should partner's hand be like on this auction?**

*You*    *Partner*
1 ♡        1 ♠
1 NT      2 ♡

Partner must have true heart support, probably three cards. He would have little reason to move away from notrump otherwise. But with 6-9 points and three hearts, he would have limited his hand immediately by raising your 1 ♡ opening to 2 ♡. This sequence should be a little stronger than a direct single raise. Partner should have a hand like:

♠ A Q 5 4 3
♡ J 8 5
◇ 6 5
♣ K 9 4

# SUMMARY

*Visualization* is a useful supplement to point-count bidding. Once partner's bidding has given you every possible bit of information, you still may have to visualize his high-card strength and distribution to assess your prospects in the play accurately.

Less experienced players concentrate only on their own cards; an expert tries to imagine how the cards lie around the table.

Good visualization requires a thorough knowledge of your bidding *system* and your partner's bidding *style*, as well as a willingness to draw inferences from *opponents' bidding*.

A good rule of thumb is:

> IF A SUITABLE MINIMUM HAND FOR PARTNER'S BIDDING WILL MAKE THE CONTRACT LAYDOWN, BID IT.

The corollary to this rule of thumb is:

> IF YOU ARE CONSIDERING A CONTRACT AND PARTNER MUST HAVE JUST THE RIGHT CARDS, FORGET IT.

**TEST YOUR COMPREHENSION OF THE MATERIAL IN THIS CHAPTER:**

I.  1.  Your hand is:    ♠ K 6 5
                            ♡ 8
                            ◊ A Q 8 6 4
                            ♣ A J 5 3

Partner responds 1 ♡ to your 1 ◊ opening and rebids 2 ♡ over 2 ♣. How many hearts should partner have? How many high-card points? What call do you make?

2.  Your hand is:  ♠ —
                   ♡ Q 7
                   ◇ K J 6 5 2
                   ♣ Q J 8 5 4 2

East opens 1 ◇ (with both sides vulnerable), West responds
1 NT, passed around to you. What distribution should your
partner have? How much high-card strength? Would you
balance with 2 ♣ ?

3.  Your hand is:  ♠ K 5
                   ♡ A K 7 6 3
                   ◇ A 8 6 4
                   ♣ A Q

East passes and you open 1 ♡. Partner raises you to 4 ♡
(preemptive). What distribution should your partner have?
Can you visualize a hand for him that would make slam
a good contract?

4.  Your hand is:  ♠ K Q 8 5
                   ♡ A J 7 5 3
                   ◇ A 6
                   ♣ A J

            *Partner*    *You*
            1 ♠          3 ♡
            4 ♡          5 ◇
            6 ♡          ?

What is partner likely to have in hearts? Assuming a grand
slam is possible, in what strain do you bid it?

5.  Your hand is:  ♠ K 7 5
                   ♡ J 5
                   ◇ 8 7 6 4
                   ♣ 9 8 6 4

West opens 1 ◇, partner cuebids 2 ◇ (strong), East bids
3 ♣, you pass, West raises to 4 ♣, partner bids 5 ♣ (!).
What do you do at your turn?

74

6.   Your hand is:   ♠ 8 6 4
                     ♡ A K 9 6
                     ◊ J 5
                     ♣ A K 4 3

| South | West | North | East |
|-------|------|-------|------|
|       |      | Pass  | 1 ♡  |
| Pass  | 1 ♠  | 2 ◊   | 2 ♠  |
| ?     |      |       |      |

What do you know about partner's hand? What call do you make?

7.   Your hand is:   ♠ K
                     ♡ J 3 2
                     ◊ A Q 7
                     ♣ A K 8 6 5 3

You open 1 ♣, West overcalls 1 ♠, partner raises to 2 ♣, East passes. What call do you make?

II.   In each sequence, give the approximate number of high-card points your partner holds and his probable distribution.

| You | Partner |
|-----|---------|
| 1.  | 1 ♡     |
| 1 ♠ | 2 ♣     |
| 2 ♡ | 2 ♠     |
|     |         |
| 2.  | 1 ◊     |
| 1 ♡ | 2 ♡     |
| 2 NT| 3 ♣     |
|     |         |
| 3.  | 1 ◊     |
| 1 ♠ | 2 ♣     |
| 2 NT| 3 ◊     |
|     |         |
| 4.  | 1 ◊     |
| 1 ♠ | 2 ◊     |
| 2 NT| 3 ♣     |

75

|  | *You* | *Partner* |
|---|---|---|
| 5. | | 1 ♢ |
| | 1 ♠ | 2 ♡ |
| | 2 NT | 3 ♠ |

|  | | |
|---|---|---|
| 6. | 1 ♠ | 2 ♢ |
| | 2 ♡ | 4 ♠ |

|  | | |
|---|---|---|
| 7. | 1 ♠ | 2 ♢ |
| | 2 ♡ | 2 ♠ |
| | 2 NT | 3 ♣ |

III.     You will be shown an auction, followed by five hands.
Pick the hand partner is most likely to hold on the bidding.

|  | *Partner* | *You* | *Opponent* |
|---|---|---|---|
| 1. | 1 ♣ | 1 ♡ | (1 ♠) |
| | Pass | | |

A    ♠ A J 7
♡ Q 6
♢ J 9 5
♣ A Q 8 5 2

B    ♠ A 8 4
♡ Q 10 5
♢ 7 6 4
♣ A K 7 4

C    ♠ A Q 9 5
♡ 5
♢ K 8 6 3
♣ A K 10 6

D    ♠ K 6 4
♡ J 6
♢ K 9 7 4
♣ A Q 10 5

E    ♠ A 7 5
♡ 8 5
♢ 10 5
♣ A K J 8 7 4

|        | *Partner* | *You* |
|--------|-----------|-------|
| 2.     | 1♣        | 1♡    |
|        | 1♠        | 2♣    |
|        | 2 NT      |       |

A   ♠ K 8 6 4       B   ♠ A K 7 5
     ♡ A 5                ♡ 4
     ◇ K 9 3             ◇ 10 6 5
     ♣ A Q J 5         ♣ A K Q 8 4

C   ♠ K J 9 3      D   ♠ K 8 7 3
     ♡ 3                  ♡ A 5
     ◇ A 8 5             ◇ K 7
     ♣ A K Q 10 5     ♣ A Q J 4 2

E   ♠ K 9 7 5
     ♡ Q 6 4
     ◇ K 9 4
     ♣ A Q 8

|        | *Partner* | *You* |
|--------|-----------|-------|
| 3.     | 1♣        | 1♡    |
|        | 2♣        | 2♠    |
|        | 3◇        |       |

A   ♠ 7 4         B   ♠ 8
     ♡ K 6               ♡ K 6 4
     ◇ A 5 3            ◇ A 7 5 3
     ♣ K Q J 9 8 4     ♣ A K J 10 4

C   ♠ 8 6         D   ♠ Q
     ♡ J 9               ♡ A
     ◇ A Q 7            ◇ A 8 6 4
     ♣ K Q J 9 6 4     ♣ Q 10 7 6 5 3 2

E   ♠ A Q 6
     ♡ 4
     ◇ 10 7 6 3
     ♣ A K J 8 6

|          | Partner | You |
|----------|---------|-----|
| 4.       |         | 1 ♡ |
|          | 1 NT    | 2 ♣ |
|          | 2 ♠     |     |

A    ♠ Q J 10 4       B.    ♠ J 9 7 6 5 3
      ♡ 9 5                  ♡ A 4
      ◇ 7 6 3              ◇ 6 4
      ♣ A Q 7 5          ♣ 8 7 5

C    ♠ A 4             D    ♠ A 6 4
      ♡ Q 7                ♡ Q 9
      ◇ 8 7 6              ◇ 8 7 5
      ♣ K 9 7 6 5 3      ♣ Q 10 7 6 4

E    ♠ A 6 4
      ♡ K Q
      ◇ 8 7 6 4
      ♣ J 10 5 4

|          | Partner | You |
|----------|---------|-----|
| 5.       | 1 ♣     | 1 ♠ |
|          | 2 NT    | 3 ♡ |
|          | 4 ◇     |     |

A    ♠ J 6 4          B    ♠ 3
      ♡ A K Q            ♡ A K 5
      ◇ A 7 4             ◇ K J 6 4
      ♣ K Q 10 5        ♣ A K J 9 2

C    ♠ 5 4             D    ♠ Q 4
      ♡ A Q               ♡ K J 6 4
      ◇ K Q 9 4          ◇ A K J
      ♣ A K J 6 3        ♣ K Q 8 3

E    ♠ K 5
      ♡ A K J 7
      ◇ A K 6
      ♣ Q 9 5 3

IV. For each bidding sequence there are four hands. Decide which hand partner is most likely to hold, and what he would have bid on the hands which do not suit the bidding sequence.

1.  | Partner | You |
    |---------|-----|
    |         | 1 ♡ |
    | 1 ♠     | 2 ◊ |
    | 2 ♡     |     |

a.  ♠ A J 6 5 3
    ♡ Q 6 4
    ◊ 7 5
    ♣ 10 4 3

b.  ♠ A J 8 5 3
    ♡ K 6 4
    ◊ Q 5
    ♣ 8 7 6

c.  ♠ Q 7 5 4 2
    ♡ K 4
    ◊ 8 7 6
    ♣ 7 6 5

d.  ♠ A J 8 6 4
    ♡ J 7
    ◊ Q 7
    ♣ 8 6 3 2

2.  | Partner | You  |
    |---------|------|
    |         | 1 ◊  |
    | 1 ♡     | 1 NT |
    | 3 ♣     | 3 ♡  |
    | 3 NT    |      |

a.  ♠ K J 4
    ♡ A Q 6 4
    ◊ 7 5
    ♣ K 7 5 3

b.  ♠ 5 4
    ♡ K Q 7 5 3
    ◊ A 5
    ♣ K 10 7 4

c.  ♠ A 5 3
    ♡ K Q 8 6 4
    ◊ Q 5
    ♣ K 10 4

d   ♠ A 4
    ♡ 10 8 6 5 3
    ◊ K 6
    ♣ A Q 7 5

79

3.
|  |  |
|---|---|
| *Partner* | *You* |
|  | 1 ♠ |
| 2 ◇ | 2 ♡ |
| 3 ♠ | 4 ♠ |
| 5 ♣ |  |

a.    ♠ 8 6 2
       ♡ Q 4
       ◇ A K Q J 9
       ♣ A 7 6

b.    ♠ K 10 7 5
       ♡ 6 5
       ◇ A K Q 7 6
       ♣ A 7

c.    ♠ A J 7 5 3
       ♡ 7 5
       ◇ K J 7 5
       ♣ A 5

d.    ♠ Q 6 5
       ♡ 5 4
       ◇ A K 7 6 5
       ♣ A K 4

4.
|  |  |
|---|---|
| *Partner* | *You* |
|  | 1 ♠ |
| 2 ♡ | 4 ♡ |
| 5 ♡ |  |

a.    ♠ 6
       ♡ Q 10 7 6 5 3
       ◇ A Q 7
       ♣ A 10 4

b.    ♠ J 5
       ♡ K Q 9 7 6 5
       ◇ 3
       ♣ A Q 7 5

c.    ♠ Q 5
       ♡ A J 10 6 4
       ◇ A J 10
       ♣ 9 6 4

d.    ♠ Q 6
       ♡ J 10 8 7 5
       ◇ A Q 8
       ♣ A 10 5

**5.**

|  | | *Partner* | | *You* |
|---|---|---|---|---|
| (1 ♡) | | Pass | (Pass) | 1 ♠ |
| (Pass) | | 3 ♣ | | |

a.  ♠ 8 7 4
    ♡ 6 4
    ◊ K 4
    ♣ A K Q 6 5 4

b.  ♠ Q 7
    ♡ K J 4
    ◊ 8 7 6
    ♣ A K J 9 4

c.  ♠ A 5
    ♡ K 5 4
    ◊ J 10 4
    ♣ A K J 7 5

d.  ♠ A 7
    ♡ 8 6 5 3
    ◊ K Q 6
    ♣ A Q J 8

**6.**

| *Partner* | *You* |
|---|---|
| 1 ♠ | 1 NT |
| 2 ♣ | 3 ♣ |
| 4 ♣ | |

a.  ♠ A J 7 5 3
    ♡ K 8
    ◊ Q 9
    ♣ A Q 9 4

b.  ♠ A K J 10 4
    ♡ 4 3
    ◊ 4 3
    ♣ A K 9 3

c.  ♠ A K Q 8 6
    ♡ 7 5
    ◊ J 5
    ♣ A 10 6 4

d.  ♠ A K J 4 3
    ♡ 4 3
    ◊ 3
    ♣ A J 9 7 6

# SOLUTIONS

I.  1.   Six or seven hearts and fewer than 10 HCP. Pass, before
         things get any worse.
    2.   Partner should have *ten* major-suit cards, since the op-
         ponents failed to find a major-suit fit. With that much
         distribution he would have acted over 1 NT with a decent
         hand. West has club length since he neither responded in
         a major nor raised diamonds. Pass.
    3.   Partner probably has a singleton or void someplace, most
         likely in diamonds, your longest suit. As little as:

         ♠ Q 10 6 4
         ♡ J 8 6 4 3
         ◇ 3
         ♣ 8 7 6

         gives you a play for slam, so you should at least try to
         get there. Even a direct 6♡ would be reasonable.
    4.   This is a famous hand. Partner must have the missing heart
         honors since he leaped to slam without the ♣A and your
         spade honors. Bid 7♡, since partner's fifth spade can pro-
         vide a crucial discard for one of your minor-suit losers.
         Partner's hand:

         ♠ A J 10 9 5
         ♡ K Q 10 5
         ◇ Q 6 5
         ♣ 5

    5.   Bid 6♠. Partner committed your side to five of a major,
         and for all he knows, you have nothing.
    6.   Partner must hold excellent diamonds — what else can
         he have when you own this much high-card strength and
         the opponents opened and responded? Cuebid 3♡ or jump
         to game in diamonds.
    7.   Bid 3 NT. West is far more likely to lead a low spade
         than to *lay down* the ♠A. A singleton king can be con-
         sidered a stopper in this situation.

II. 1.   3-5-1-4 pattern (rarely, 3-5-2-3). About 16-17 HCP. Partner's sequence shows game interest despite your (weak) preference.

2.   1-3-5-4 pattern. 12-13 HCP. Discouraging game *and* notrump.

3.   Six or seven diamonds, four clubs. About 15-17 HCP. This sequence suggest extra values.

4.   Six or seven diamonds, four clubs. About 11-14 HCP. This sequence suggests a minimum.

5.   3-4-5-1 pattern (rarely, 3-4-4-2 or 3-3-5-2). 17+ HCP. This is a *forcing* sequence.

6.   Five or six diamonds, four spades. About 13-15 HCP. Suggests good diamonds and good spades.

7.   3-1-5-4 pattern (perhaps 3-0-5-5). About 11-12 HCP.

III. 1.   D is correct.
A would rebid 1 NT freely.
B should raise 1 ♡ to 2 ♡.
C would double 1 ♠.
E would rebid 2 ♣.

2.   D is correct.
A would open 1 NT.
B would try for game with 3 ♣.
C would try with 2 ◇.
E would pass 2 ♣.

3.   A is correct.
B would take a heart preference over 2 ♠.
C would bid notrump over 2 ♠.
D would bid clubs *again*.
E should raise 2 ♠ to 3 ♠.

4.   C is correct.
A would respond 1 ♠ to 1 ♡.
B also would respond 1 ♠ to 1 ♡.
D would raise 2 ♣ to 3 ♣.
E would raise clubs or jump to 3 ♡.
(2 ♠ here is a strange bid — it shows a hand that is improved because of partner's rebid.)

5. E is correct.
A would take a spade preference over 3♡.
B would rebid 2◇, not 2 NT.
C would bid 3 NT over 3♡.
D would raise 3♡ to 4♡.
(4◇ is an *advance cuebid*, implying a maximum hand and excellent hearts.)

IV. 1. a. Raise 1♡ to 2♡.
b. Jump to 3♡ (invitational) over 2◇.
c. Might pass 1♡. Do not risk a second bid over 2◇.
d. Fits the sequence.
2. a. Raise 1 NT to 3 NT.
b. With good hearts, raise 3♡ to 4♡.
c. Probably raise 1 NT to 3 NT.
d. Fits the sequence. Five bad hearts, semi-balanced hand.
3. a. Do not try for slam with bad spades; pass 4♠.
b. Jump shift to 3◇ over 1♠.
c. Raise spades directly. Do not act over 4♠ with a minimum in high cards.
d. Fits the sequence.
4. a. Bid 6♡ over 4♡.
b. Use Blackwood over 4♡.
c. Try for slam with a 5◇ cuebid.
d. Fits the sequence (which asks for help in hearts and promises minor-suit controls.)
5. a. Overcall 2♣.
b. Overcall to begin with. If not, bid 2 NT over 1♠.
c. Overcall 1 NT.
d. Fits the sequence. (Some players would cuebid 2♡ with this hand, however.)

6.   a.   Bid 3 NT over 3♣.
     b.   Bid 3♠ over 3♣.
     c.   Pass 3♣.
     d.   Fits the sequence. Partner is probably 5-5 since he made no more descriptive game try.

# Chapter 6

## FINE POINTS OF DECLARER PLAY: TECHNIQUE

Let's look at a hand that illustrates *technique* in declarer play.

♠ 8 6 4
♡ A 5
♢ A J 4 3 2
♣ K 3 2

♠ Q 9 3
♡ K Q 10 7 6 4
♢ 5
♣ A Q 6

You, South, are declarer in 4 ♡. Partner opened 1 ♢ , you responded 1 ♡ , he rebid 1 NT, you leaped to 4 ♡. West leads the ♠ 2. East wins the ace and returns a spade. West takes the jack and king and shifts to a club. **Plan the play.**

The only possible problem is in trumps. You can do nothing if West has J-9-x-x, but if East has that holding, you may be able to engineer a TRUMP COUP against him. If you arrive in dummy at trick 12 with these cards:

♠ —
♡ —
♢ J 4
♣ —

♠ —
♡ Q 10
♢ —
♣ —

you can pick up East's trumps as though with a finesse. The trump coup requires you to *shorten* yourself in trumps to the same length as East. If you lack entries to dummy, as you do here, you need to begin the shortening process before you learn that it's necessary. Proper technique is: win the club shift in hand, diamond to the ace, diamond ruff. Now king and ace of trumps. If West shows out, ruff another diamond, and play the ♣Q and a club to the king. If East can't ruff in, you will be in dummy in the desired position at trick 12. Note that if you fail to ruff a diamond before playing trumps, you will be an entry short to ruff yourself down to the right length.

This deal illustrates an essential ingredient for the good technician: *foresight*. Good technique means foreseeing developments in the play and catering to as many as possible.

Technical proficiency in declarer play has many aspects. There are the coups, the loser-on-loser plays, the endplays. Some hands require you to combine chances, manage your entries, set up a suit or time the play correctly. We will look at three important areas that require technical ability.

| | |
|---|---|
| 1. | TRUMP CONTROL AND TRUMP MANAGEMENT |
| 2. | PERCENTAGE PLAY |
| 3. | SQUEEZE PLAY |

# 1. TRUMP CONTROL AND TRUMP MANAGEMENT

In any trump contract, declarer must draw trumps before he can safely cash side-suit winners. A tenuous trump holding can make it hard to do this and keep control of the play. A typical situation occurs when declarer lands in a 4-3 fit:

1.
        ♠ A 10 3
        ♡ A Q 4 3
        ◇ 5 4 3
        ♣ 4 3 2

        ♠ K Q J 4
        ♡ K 7 2
        ◇ 8 7
        ♣ A K Q 7

You, South, opened 1 ♣, North responded 1 ♡. You rebid 1 ♠, North (with an uncomfortable problem) raised to 2 ♠. You jumped to 4 ♠. West leads the ◇ K and continues the suit. **How should you play?**

The safest plan is to *discard* on the third round of diamonds instead of letting yourself be ruffed down to three trumps. If the opponents lead a fourth diamond, you can ruff in dummy, preserving the four trumps in your hand. *Refusal to ruff* is a common method of keeping control. Often, you will have a *sure loser* you can discard instead of ruffing. This is called a loser-on-loser play.

2.
        ♠ A 4
        ♡ Q 8 6 5
        ◇ A K 4 3
        ♣ A 8 7

        ♠ K Q J 10 8 5
        ♡ 7 4 3 2
        ◇ 9 7
        ♣ Q

You, South, are declarer in 4 ♠. North opened 1 NT, you jumped to game. The opening lead is the ♣ J, and you win dummy's ace. **How should you play?**

You need a heart trick and you will require a 3-2 split. Suppose you begin by drawing trumps. If trumps are 3-2, you will have three left so you can afford to give the opponents the lead three times with heart tricks and still keep control. But if trumps go 4-1 (a 28% chance), you will be in trouble. The opponents will force you out of control with repeated club leads, and you will never get your heart trick. Since you probably need a 3-2 heart split anyhow, lead a heart from dummy at trick two. The defense will win and force you to ruff a club. You concede another heart. They force you again. You concede a third heart, establishing the fourth heart. If the opponents lead another club now, *dummy* can ruff, and you can keep four trumps in your hand and keep control.

A sound principle of play, illustrated here, applies to many hands.

---

WHEN THE HAND LOOKS TOUGH, A GOOD FIRST MOVE IS TO *ESTABLISH YOUR SIDE SUIT.*

---

3.
    ♠ K 10 4
    ♡ 6 5 4
    ◊ A 7
    ♣ A J 8 6 4

    ♠ A Q 5 3
    ♡ A 8 3
    ◊ 6 5 4
    ♣ K Q 7

You, South, opened 1 ♣ and partner responded 3 ♣. You tried 3 ♠ and partner raised to 4 ♠ (even though 3 NT is cold). You decided you could handle a 4-3 fit and passed. The opening lead is the ◊ Q. You win, fearing a heart switch. **How should you continue?**

You can make this contract if you can get all your club tricks. But if you draw three rounds of trumps and find a defender with a trump trick, he may ruff in before you can cash your clubs, leaving you stranded with losers. Note that *you have ten winners even if you lose a trick in trumps.* The solution, therefore, is to *concede a trump trick* early. Lead a trump from dummy and *duck.* You can win the return (if they lead diamonds, *dummy* can ruff), draw three more rounds of trumps, and run your clubs safely.

The last hand was more a matter of trump *management* than control. Here is another.

4.
&spades; A 7 5 3
&hearts; 7 5 4
&diams; 7 6 4
&clubs; A 6 4

&spades; 9
&hearts; A Q J
&diams; A K Q 3
&clubs; J 8 7 5 2

You, South, arrive at a poor 5 &clubs; (partner's fault). West leads the &clubs; Q, and you win. **How do you play?**

Of course, you will need the heart finesse and a 3-2 club break, but you also have your fourth diamond to worry about. You can ruff it in dummy if necessary, but you cannot do so without drawing any trumps — you might lose an extra trump trick on an overruff. Your plan should be to draw *two* rounds of trumps and then take your other tricks, leaving the opponents with a single high trump that they can have whenever they want it. To do this, *duck the first round* of trumps and play your ace next.

Since entries to dummy are scarce, take the heart finesse at trick two. Then play a low trump from both hands. Ruff the spade return, play a club to the ace, take another heart finesse and cash your diamonds, ruffing the fourth round if necessary. The opponents will take only two trump tricks. You need luck to make this contract; but if your luck is in, you must be able to take advantage!

## 2. PERCENTAGE PLAY

Sometimes you must choose a line of play strictly on a mathematical basis. Although a knowledge of probability is not essential to winning bridge, knowing the likely division of missing cards can be helpful. The table below lists these odds.

### A GUIDE TO PERCENTAGES

| Number of missing cards | Break | Odds |
|---|---|---|
| 2 | 1-1 | 52 % |
|  | 2-0 | 48 |
| 3 | 2-1 | 78 |
|  | 3-0 | 22 |
| 4 | 3-1 | 49.7 |
|  | 2-2 | 40.7 |
|  | 4-0 | 9.6 |
| 5 | 3-2 | 67.8 |
|  | 4-1 | 28.3 |
|  | 5-0 | 3.9 |
| 6 | 4-2 | 48.4 |
|  | 3-3 | 35.5 |
|  | 5-1 | 14.5 |
|  | 6-0 | 1.5 |
| 7 | 4-3 | 62.6 |
|  | 5-2 | 30.5 |
|  | 6-1 | 6.8 |
|  | 7-0 | .5 |
| 8 | 5-3 | 47.1 |
|  | 4-4 | 32.7 |
|  | 6-2 | 17.1 |
|  | 7-1 | 2.9 |
|  | 8-0 | .2 |

You should bear these points in mind:

> 1. RELY ON PERCENTAGES *ONLY* WHEN TECH-NIQUES OF COUNTING, INFERENCE AND TABLE PRESENCE ARE INADEQUATE.
> 2. THE ODDS OF A PARTICULAR DIVISION OF OUTSTANDING CARDS WILL *CHANGE* DURING THE PLAY. SOME DIVISIONS WILL BECOME IM-POSSIBLE. THE ODDS ON THE ALTERNATIVE DIVISIONS WILL THEREFORE INCREASE PROPORTIONATELY.

If you're unwilling to memorize a percentage table, remembering this will help:

> AN *ODD* NUMBER OF OUTSTANDING CARDS WILL TEND TO BREAK AS EVENLY AS POSSIBLE. AN *EVEN* NUMBER OF OUTSTANDING CARDS WILL TEND TO BREAK UNEVENLY.

Let's look at some deals that illustrate simple percentage play.

5.
♠ A K Q
♡ 6 5
◊ A K Q 3 2
♣ A Q 2

♠ 5 4 3 2
♡ A 8
◊ 5 4
♣ 8 7 6 5 4

You, South, are declarer in 3 NT. West leads the ♡Q, and you win your ace right away. **How do you proceed?**

You have eight top tricks and can get a ninth one from either a 3-3 diamond split or a winning club finesse. Since a 3-3 split is less than an even chance (35.5%), the club finesse is your best bet.

6.
    ♠ A 6 5 4 3
    ♡ 4
    ◊ A 4 3 2
    ♣ 4 3 2

    ♠ 8
    ♡ A Q J 10 5 3
    ◊ 7 6 5
    ♣ A Q J

You, South, are declarer in 4♡. The opening lead is the ♠K, which you win. **How do you play?**

Clearly, it is right to take the *club* finesse. A winning heart finesse may gain nothing, since you would still have to find East's king guarded only once. If your club finesse works, you will play the ♡A and continue trumps, intending to repeat the club finesse when you use your other entry to dummy.

7.
    ♠ K
    ♡ A K Q 7 5 3
    ◊ 6 5 3
    ♣ A Q 7

    ♠ A J 10 4
    ♡ 9 6 2
    ◊ J 8 2
    ♣ J 6 2

You, South, are declarer in 3 NT. The defenders cash four diamond tricks, ending in the East hand, and shift to a spade. **How do you play?**

You have two options:
(1) Overtake the ♠K with the ace and finesse in clubs. This is a 50% shot.
(2) Win the ♠K and cash two high hearts. If the hearts are 2-2, you gain entry to hand with the ♡9 and win the ♠A for your ninth trick.

Since a 2-2 heart split is less than an even chance, the first line of play is better.

(Note: *At matchpoint duplicate,* the choice would be more difficult, since line (1) will lead to down *two* if it fails. Also a factor is the fate of the 4 ♡ contract that will be reached at many tables.)

*AN UNDERSTANDING OF THE PRINCIPLE OF RESTRICTED CHOICE WILL EARN YOU MANY EXTRA TRICKS AND THE RESPECT OF YOUR PARTNER.*

The Principle of *Restricted Choice*

This is an elusive and interesting mathematical concept that can be applied to the play of certain suit combinations. The best way to explain the Principle is by example. Suppose you are playing 7 ♠ with this trump suit:

♠ A 4 3 2

♠ K 10 9 6 5

The opponents did not bid, and you have no clue to the lie of the trumps. You lead a trump to dummy's ace, and West plays an *honor* (either one), East plays the *seven*. When you lead a spade back, East plays the *eight*. **What should you do?**

In fact, it is correct to *finesse* your ten, playing West for a singleton honor. The odds in your favor are heavy. Consider this: If West held the doubleton Q-J, he would have a choice of equal cards to play from. Presumably, he would play at random; the queen on some occasions, the jack on others.

> SINCE WEST DID, IN FACT, PLAY ONE HONOR, THE PRESUMPTION IS THAT HE DOES *NOT* HAVE Q-J DOUBLETON; IF HE DID, HE MIGHT HAVE PLAYED HIS *OTHER* HONOR.

This may sound like a fantasy, but it has a sound mathematical basis; and, even more important, it usually works! Let's look at another situation where Restricted Choice applies.

A 3 2

K Q 8 4

You are declarer, needing four tricks from this suit and having no clues from the bidding or play. You cash the king and ace, and West plays the nine and jack. The odds heavily favor a *finesse of the eight* on the third round. If West had the J-10-9, he could have played his equals in several ways. But if he held J-9, his choice of plays would have been restricted to his actual play.

8.  ♠ K 3 2
    ♡ 5 4 3 2
    ◇ 4 3 2
    ♣ Q 3 2

    ♠ A Q 4
    ♡ A K 6
    ◇ Q 7 6
    ♣ A K 9 4

You, South, are declarer in 3 NT. The opening lead is the ♠J. Both opponents follow to three rounds of spades and the ♡A and ♡K. You continue with the ♣A and a club to the queen. West plays the *ten* on the second round. East follows low when you return a club toward your hand. **What card do you play?**

Right, the ♣9, applying the Principle of Restricted Choice. With J-10-x West might have played his *jack* on the second round of clubs.

## 3. SQUEEZE PLAY

This is a brief look at a subject of formidable complexity. A hand contains some cards that are *busy*, representing a trick or a stopper, and some that are relatively worthless, or *idle*. When a player must discard a busy card (because he has nothing else), he is said to be *squeezed*. A squeeze is a way an expert declarer can create extra tricks.

While there are many types of squeezes, and executing some of the more advanced types can be difficult, a few basic principles apply to most squeezes, and certainly to the simple types of squeezes we will discuss.

1.  The same opponent must hold busy cards in *more than one suit*.
2.  Declarer must have *threat cards* (cards that threaten to become winners), and the threats must be accompanied by *entries*.
3.  Declarer's threat cards must be so *positioned* that the squeeze will operate.
4.  In basic squeeze positions, the *count must be rectified*. That is, declarer must have only one loser remaining, which the squeeze will let him avoid. To rectify the count, declarer may have to lose tricks deliberately.
5.  To operate the squeeze, declarer must play *every one* of his winners outside the suit involved in the squeeze. Refrain from cashing that last trump, for instance, and the squeeze will fail.

Here is a matrix of cards that illustrates a squeeze position:

♠ A J
♡ K
♢ —
♣ —

♠ K Q
♡ A
♢ —
♣ —

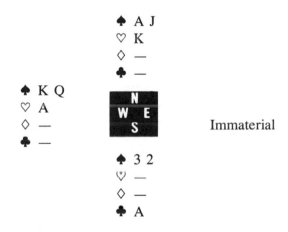

Immaterial

♠ 3 2
♡ —
♢ —
♣ A

South is declarer at notrump, needing the last three tricks. He leads the ♣ A. West must discard before dummy and cannot avoid losing a trick whatever he discards. Note that:

1. West holds busy cards in two suits.
2. Dummy has threat cards, the ♠ J and ♡ K.
3. Dummy's threats are positioned well, since dummy plays after West. (This condition is not essential for all squeezes, but it makes this squeeze easier.)
4. The count is rectified — declarer has all the tricks *but one*.
5. The squeeze works as declarer plays his *last* winner outside the squeeze suits.

97

Here is a deal that illustrates a simple squeeze:

9.
           ♠ A 7 6 5 4 3
           ♡ A
           ◇ K J
           ♣ A Q J 3

           ♠ K 8
           ♡ Q 6 5
           ◇ A Q 10 9 4
           ♣ K 7 6

You, South, reach a 7 NT contract, and West leads the ♣ 10. **How do you play?**

You have 12 top tricks and no chance for a 13th other than a squeeze. The trick to skillful squeeze play is often to *visualize the position at the end of the hand, when the squeeze takes effect.* Here, your last three cards will be:

           ♠ A 7 6
           ♡ —
           ◇ —
           ♣ —

           ♠ K 8
           ♡ Q
           ◇ —
           ♣ —

If *either* opponent has the ♡ K plus three or more spades, he will be unable to discard effectively to trick ten. This hand illustrates the most elementary type of squeeze — indeed, it is called a SIMPLE squeeze.

# SUMMARY

Good technique as declarer means *foreseeing* possible developments in the play and catering to as many of them as you can.

## I. TRUMP CONTROL AND TRUMP MANAGEMENT

In most trump contracts declarer must draw trumps before he can safely cash side-suit winners. If his trump holding is ragged or shorter than usual, he may have trouble keeping *control*. Some points declarer should keep in mind:

1. When the play appears to be full of problems and trump control may be difficult, *a good first move is to establish a side suit.*
2. Declarer may be able to counter a forcing defense effectively by refusing to ruff — perhaps by making a *loser-on-loser* play.
3. In managing his trumps, declarer often wants to *leave a single high trump outstanding* while he goes about his other business.

## II. PERCENTAGE PLAY

Often the only way to choose from among possible lines of play is on a mathematical basis. A knowledge of the odds on the common suit divisions can be helpful.

A GOOD RULE OF THUMB: AN ODD NUMBER OF OUTSTANDING CARDS WILL TEND TO DIVIDE AS EVENLY AS POSSIBLE, WHILE AN EVEN NUMBER OF OUTSTANDING CARDS WILL TEND TO DIVIDE UNEVENLY.

## III. SQUEEZE PLAY

A bridge hand contains some cards that are *busy,* representing tricks or stoppers, and some cards that are relatively worthless, or *idle.* When a player is forced to discard a busy card, he is said to be *squeezed.* While many types of squeezes exist, some of formidable complexity, a few principles apply to almost all squeezes and especially to the basic positions.

1. One opponent must hold busy cards in *more than one suit.*
2. Declarer must have *threat cards* (cards that threaten to become winners) and they must be accompanied by *entries.*
3. Declarer's threat cards must be so *placed* that the squeeze will function.
4. In the basic squeeze positions, the *count must be rectified.* Declarer must have only one remaining loser. To rectify the count, declarer may have to lose a trick or tricks on purpose.

To operate the squeeze, declarer should:

1. *Visualize* the position of the cards when the squeeze takes effect.
2. Cash all his winners outside the suits involved in the squeeze. Declarer must not be afraid to part with (for instance) his last trump in trying for a squeeze.

**TEST YOUR COMPREHENSION OF THE MATERIAL IN THIS CHAPTER:**

1.
♠ 6 5
♡ 10 5 4 2
♢ A K 4 3
♣ K 5 4

♠ A 8 4 3
♡ A 7 6 3
♢ J 2
♣ A Q 2

You are declarer in 4♡. West leads the ♠2, East plays the king. Plan the play.

2.
                ♠ A
                ♡ K Q
                ◊ A K 4 3 2
                ♣ J 5 4 3 2

                ♠ K Q J 10 2
                ♡ A 8 7 6 5
                ◊ 6 5
                ♣ 7

You are declarer in 4 ♡. West leads the ♣ 10, which holds, and continues with a second club, which you ruff. Plan the play.

3.
                ♠ A J 2
                ♡ K 2
                ◊ A K 3 2
                ♣ J 4 3 2

                ♠ 3
                ♡ A Q J 10 4 3
                ◊ 5 4
                ♣ 8 7 6 5

You are declarer in 4 ♡. West leads the ♠ 10, won by dummy's ace. How do you continue?

4.
                ♠ 3 2
                ♡ A K Q J 10
                ◊ 2
                ♣ A 7 6 5 4

                ♠ A K 7 6 5 4
                ♡ 3 2
                ◊ A 7 6 5
                ♣ 8

You are declarer in 6 ♠. West leads the ◊ K. Plan the play.

5. ♠ 4 3 2
  ♡ A 5
  ◇ K J 3 2
  ♣ K Q 8 7

  ♠ A K Q
  ♡ 7 4
  ◇ A 7
  ♣ A J 9 5 4 3

You are declarer in 7♣. West leads the ♡K. What is the best percentage play for the contract?

6.

  ♠ 5 4
  ♡ A Q 9 3
  ◇ 6 5 4
  ♣ K 4 3 2

  ♠ A 9
  ♡ J 10 4
  ◇ A K J 10 3
  ♣ A 6 5

You are declarer in 3 NT. West leads the ♠6, East playing the queen. Plan the play.

7. ♠ K 9 7
  ♡ A 3 2
  ◇ K 10 8 4
  ♣ K J 10

  ♠ A Q J 10 8 3
  ♡ K 7 6
  ◇ A 9 3
  ♣ 6

You are declarer in 6♠ after East opened 3♣. West leads a club to East's queen, and you ruff the ♣A, as West follows. You draw trumps in two rounds and cash the ◇A and ◇K, with West playing the jack on the second round. Next you cash the ♣K, pitching a diamond, and West follows. How do you continue?

8.

       ♠ A 5
       ♡ Q 4 3
       ♢ A 7 6 5 4
       ♣ K 6 4

       ♠ J 7 3
       ♡ A K 8
       ♢ 9 8 3
       ♣ A Q 9 3

You are declarer in 3 NT. West leads the ♠6. East wins the queen and returns the nine to dummy's ace. You play a club to your ace and a club back to the king. West follows with the ten on this trick. When you lead a third club, East follows low. What card do you play from your hand?

9.

       ♠ 5 4 3
       ♡ A 3 2
       ♢ J 4 3
       ♣ Q 7 6 5

       ♠ K Q J 9 8 7 6
       ♡ K J 7
       ♢ 8 6
       ♣ A

West opened 1 ♢, North and East passed, you bid 4 ♠. West leads the three top diamonds, and you ruff the third round. The ♠K is won by East, who returns the ♡10. Plan the play.

10.　　　　　　♠ A K 9 2
　　　　　　　♡ 10 3 2
　　　　　　　◇ K 3 2
　　　　　　　♣ A 4 3

　　　　　　　♠ 5 4
　　　　　　　♡ A K Q J 5
　　　　　　　◇ A 8
　　　　　　　♣ K Q 6 5

You are declarer in 7 NT. West leads the ♠Q. Plan the play.

## SOLUTIONS

1.  You want to draw just two rounds of trumps and then crossruff, leaving the single high trump out. Concede the first round of trumps and play the ace next. The defense will be unable to draw a damaging third round of trumps. Also, you should duck the opening lead so the defenders cannot win their spade trick at a point when they could cash a high trump.

2.  Play a heart to the king, cash the ♠A and overtake the ♡Q with your ace. Then begin to run your spades. The defense will take two trump tricks and one club. Any other line of play risks losing control of trumps.

3.  If you draw trumps immediately and find a 4-1 break, you won't have time to set up the club trick you need. Repeated spade leads will force you out of control. You must lead a club at trick two. The defense will win and force you again. When you concede the third club, the dummy will be out of spades — you can preserve the trump length in your hand and hope to keep control (and score your established club) against normal breaks.

4.  Win the ◇A and *duck a trump*. You can win any return and hope to draw trumps so you can run your hearts without interruption.

5.  Take the diamond *finesse*. This is superior to trying to ruff out the ◇Q.

6.  Cash the ◇ A and ◇ K. If the queen falls, you have nine tricks. If not, fall back on the heart finesse. The two chances combined are greater than the chance that a single red-suit finesse will work.

7. East had six clubs, two spades and at least two diamonds. Play the ♡K and ♡A to see what you can learn about the heart distribution. As it happens, East shows out on the second heart, so you can count him for 2-1-4-6 pattern — a ruffing finesse in diamonds is a sure thing. (Percentages are nice, counting is even better.)

8. Play the ♣9. This is a Restricted-Choice position.

9. Win the ♡K, preserving dummy's ace as an entry, and run all your spades. West must have the ♣K and ♡Q when East shows up with the ♠A (East passed partner's opening bid, remember), so West will be squeezed in hearts and clubs.

10. Win and cash your club honors. If West has a stopper, you can run all your heart and diamond tricks and squeeze him in clubs and spades. If East controls clubs, you run your hearts for a double squeeze. Neither opponent will be able to keep a diamond guard.

# Chapter 7

## BIDDING OVER A TAKEOUT DOUBLE; YOUR COMPETITIVE JUDGMENT

Good competitive judgment can best be developed through long experience at the table, not from reading a book. Nevertheless, we will look at some *principles* a good player uses in making judgment decisions. We can also look at ways he can avoid being forced to *guess* in competitive auctions.

Even an expert goes wrong part of the time, of course. Consistency in competitive judgment should be your goal.

To begin, let's look at a common situation that will bring on a competitive action:

*YOUR COMPETITIVE JUDGMENT WILL IMPROVE WITH PRACTICE.*

# I. BIDDING OVER A TAKEOUT DOUBLE

We mean *their* takeout double, not your partner's. In choosing an action when partner's opening bid is doubled for takeout, keep these ideas in mind:

1. Since the auction has turned competitive, your side will have to judge where and how high to compete. Giving partner a clear description of your hand early in the auction may help him judge correctly.
2. You have less reason to suggest a weak major suit as trumps. Presumably, the takeout doubler has support for the unbid suits, especially the majors.
3. A redouble isn't always the best action if you hold 10 HCP or more. If you have a hand with offensive potential, with several features to describe, spending a round of bidding to redouble is shortsighted.

Partner opens 1 ♡ with neither side vulnerable, and right-hand opponent doubles. **What do you call with these hands?**

1. ♠ Q 7 5　　　　　　　Pass.
   ♡ Q 7 5 3
   ◇ 7 5 3
   ♣ 6 5 3

2. ♠ 5 4　　　　　　　2♡. The bid you would make without
   ♡ Q 6 5　　　　　　the double.
   ◇ A 8 6 4
   ♣ 7 6 5 3

3. ♠ 4　　　　　　　　3♡. A double raise is now *preemptive,*
   ♡ Q 8 6 4　　　　　since you would redouble with most
   ◇ Q J 7 4　　　　　strong hands.
   ♣ 8 6 5 4

4. ♠ 4　　　　　　　　4♡. This is also preemptive.
   ♡ K J 7 5 3
   ◇ Q 10 6 5 3
   ♣ 8 6

5. ♠ 7 5
   ♡ Q 7 5
   ◇ K 6 4 3
   ♣ A 8 6 4

   Pass and raise hearts at your next turn. This is a way to distinguish between a maximum and minimum raise to 2 ♡ over a takeout double.

6. ♠ K 6 4
   ♡ Q 8
   ◇ K 8 6 4
   ♣ 9 5 4 2

   1 NT. Make your normal response.

7. ♠ K 10 6 4
   ♡ Q 6
   ◇ K 8 6
   ♣ 10 7 6 4

   1 NT. You would respond 1 ♠ without the double, but now it is better to make one bid that describes your hand. The takeout doubler probably has spades, so even if your side has a spade fit, you may run into a bad split.

8. ♠ J 8 6 4
   ♡ 7
   ◇ A J 5 4
   ♣ Q 7 6 4

   Pass. There is no good bid. 1 NT would promise a balanced hand with heart tolerance. (Some players might try 1 ♠, hoping to locate a good contract. Perhaps opener would rebid two of a minor.)

9. ♠ K Q 9 5 3
   ♡ 7 6
   ◇ Q 6
   ♣ 9 5 4 2

   1 ♠. A reasonable rule is to avoid bidding a suit you wouldn't like to see partner lead. Incidentally, most pairs play this one-level response as *forcing*.

10. ♠ 5
    ♡ Q 8
    ◇ K Q 8 6 5 4
    ♣ J 7 6 5

    2 ◇. You need a good suit or hand to bid at the two level. However, many pairs play a two-level response as *not* forcing.

11. ♠ 4
    ♡ J 7
    ◇ 8 7 6
    ♣ K J 10 8 6 5 4

    3 ♣. A jump shift is *preemptive*, since you would start with a redouble if your hand were strong.

12. ♠ K Q 6 3      Redouble. If they run to diamonds or
    ♡ J 8         spades, you may double. If they run
    ◊ A J 7 6 5   to clubs, perhaps partner can double.
    ♣ 7 6

13. ♠ K Q 6 5     A *pass* is a good tactic here. The op-
    ♡ 5           ponents may unsuspectingly or un-
    ◊ A Q 7 6     wisely bid too much, and you can
    ♣ Q 9 8 6     double for a bigger penalty. Note that
                  you can double any suit yourself — you
don't need to get partner's cooperation by starting with a redouble.

14. ♠ 5 4         Redouble and support hearts next.
    ♡ K Q 7 6
    ◊ A 6 5
    ♣ J 7 6 5

15. ♠ 6 5         Redouble and jump in hearts next.
    ♡ K Q 7 6
    ◊ A Q 7 6
    ♣ Q 5 4

16. ♠ A K 6       Redouble and bid diamonds next.
    ♡ 6 5
    ◊ K Q 10 7 6 5
    ♣ Q 6

17. ♠ 5          This situation can be handled with a
    ♡ K 7 6 4     *convention* known as *Jordan*. A
    ◊ A Q 7 6     *2 NT response* shows an invitational
    ♣ 9 7 6 5     hand with good heart support and
                  distribution. Note that 2 NT cannot be
natural — you would start with a redouble if you held a strong
balanced hand. Although you have the values to redouble, 2 NT is
a better tactical action because the opponents will have a harder time
bidding spades.

Partner opens 1♣ with neither side vulnerable, and RHO doubles. What do you call with these hands?

18. ♠ 6 5
    ♡ K 6 5
    ◇ A J 10 6 5
    ♣ 6 5 4

    1◇.

19. ♠ 4 3
    ♡ A Q 10 6 5
    ◇ 8 7
    ♣ K J 6 4

    1♡. For a discussion of this situation, see Chapter 3 — redoubles.

20. ♠ K 6 5
    ♡ Q 10 7 6
    ◇ K 6 5
    ♣ J 6 5

    1 NT. We suggest you shelve the hearts and describe your hand.

21. ♠ K Q J 4
    ♡ 6 5
    ◇ J 8 6 5
    ♣ 9 8 7

    1♠, if only for lead-directing purposes.

22. ♠ 5 4
    ♡ A 7 6 5
    ◇ 8 7 6
    ♣ K J 9 6

    2♣. You likely will bid only once, so make the bid that describes your hand.

23. ♠ 4
    ♡ Q 10 6 5
    ◇ 8 7 6
    ♣ Q J 7 6 5

    3♣. Preemptive.

24. ♠ —
    ♡ Q 7 6
    ◇ 8 7 6 5
    ♣ Q 10 7 6 5 3

    4♣, even more preemptive!

## II. MORE COMPETITIVE AUCTIONS

**1. Free bids and free raises**. The *free bid principle* states that when you act in a situation where passing to partner is an option, you need a *sound* basis for your *free bid*. Suppose you hold:

♠ A 7 6
♡ Q 6
◇ K 8 6 3
♣ K J 6 5

You are dealer and open 1 ♣. Partner responds 1 ♡, so you must rebid 1 NT. But suppose RHO overcalls 1 ♠. You can describe your hand well now with a *pass*. You suggest that your opening is minimum and you have nothing special you want to say. If partner has a good hand, he will not let the auction die. To rebid 1 NT *freely*, you need a maximum hand for your bid, close to 15 HCP.

However, this idea does not apply to *raising* partner. If you have support for his suit, you must show it even with a high-card minimum. Say you hold:

♠ Λ 7 6
♡ K 7 6 5
◇ 8 7
♣ A J 7 6

You open 1 ♣, partner responds 1 ♡, and there is a 1 ♠ overcall. You cannot suppress your heart support and must raise to 2 ♡. Many players, in the absence of certain conventional methods, would raise here with only a tolerance for partner's suit — they would make the same 2 ♡ bid with:

♠ A 7 6
♡ K 7 6
◇ 8 7
♣ A J 6 5 4

The bottom line is that the often-heard term *free raise* is really meaningless.

The idea of passing to partner when you have no clearcut action also applies to . . .

**2. Forcing passes.** There are many situations where you can pass, confident that partner will act further, and let him use his judgment. Suppose, for example, that you hold:

♠ A Q 7 6 5
♡ A 7 6
◇ 8 7
♣ K 8 7

Neither side is vulnerable. You open 1 ♠, and partner responds 3 ♠ (forcing). Right-hand opponent overcalls 4 ◇. Why not pass this around? Partner can always bid 4 ♠ (he must do *something*), but he may be happy to double for penalty.

♠ A K Q 9 5 4
♡ A K 8
◇ A Q 6
♣ 5

Again, no one is vulnerable. You open 2 ♣, partner responds 2 ◇ (negative), you rebid 2 ♠ and he says 2 NT. Now RHO bids 3 ♣. Pass. If partner can double, you will happily pass again.

**3. When partner's opening bid is overcalled with 1 NT.**

With 9 or more HCP, you should usually *double* for penalty. Any other action denies that much strength, and jump responses are preemptive.

Partner opens 1 ♠, RHO overcalls 1 NT. **What do you call with these hands, with no one vulnerable?**

25.  ♠ Q 7 6 4          2 ♠, your normal action.
     ♡ A 7 6 5
     ◇ 5 4
     ♣ 8 7 6

26. ♠ A 7 6 5       Double.
     ♡ A K 7 6
     ◊ J 7
     ♣ 8 7 6

27. ♠ 6 5          Double.
     ♡ A 7 6
     ◊ 8 7 5
     ♣ A Q 7 6 5

28. ♠ 6 5          2♣.
     ♡ 8 7
     ◊ 8 7 6
     ♣ K Q J 7 6 5

29. ♠ J 9 6 5 3      3♠. Preemptive.
     ♡ 8
     ◊ Q 9 8 7
     ♣ 9 8 7

30. ♠ 7 6          3◊. Preemptive.
     ♡ 6
     ◊ K J 10 9 8 7 6
     ♣ J 8 7

## 4. When the opponents preempt.

Preemptive action by the opponents, especially opening preempts, can cause all kinds of headaches. That's why preempts are so popular. They work! If they open with a preempt in front of you, keep these ideas in mind:

> 1. To bid accurately with less room in the auction, *base any action on the assumption that partner has 6 or more HCP.* (In responding, your partner should bear in mind that you are assuming he has a few values.)
> 2. *Strain to enter the auction when you are short in the preempter's suit.*

With neither side vulnerable, RHO deals and opens 3 ♡. What do you call with these hands?

31. ♠ 7 6 5          Bid 3 NT.
    ♡ K 7 6
    ◇ A K Q 7 6
    ♣ A K

32. ♠ A K J 7 6 5     Bid 3 ♠. You would prefer to have
    ♡ 8 7            more and you could easily be doubled
    ◇ K Q 5          for a heavy set. Preempts are bound to
    ♣ J 3            get you some of the time.

33. ♠ A 7 6 5         This is a minimum takeout double. You
    ♡ 8             would prefer to have a few more
    ◇ K Q 6 5         points.
    ♣ A J 7 6

34. ♠ J 7 3           Bid 4 ◇. You are weak in high cards,
    ♡ —             but to pass with a heart void is bad
    ◇ K Q 10 8 6 5 3    tactics.
    ♣ A J 6

With neither side vulnerable, RHO deals and opens 4 ♠. What do you call with these hands?

35. ♠ A 4 3           Double. This is for *penalty*. Partner
    ♡ K 6 5          can bid, but he is on his own.
    ◇ A K 7 6 4
    ♣ A 3

36. ♠ —             Bid *4 NT*. This is played as a giant
    ♡ K Q 8 7         takeout double and asks partner to pick
    ◇ A K 7 6 5       a suit. Most pairs play that 4 NT pro-
    ♣ K Q 6 5         mises support for all the unbid suits.
                    A few play that it promises length only
                    in the minors or any two unbid suits.

114

## III. YOUR COMPETITIVE JUDGMENT

The auction will be competitive when *both* sides have a good trump suit and a share of the high-card strength. In such a case, you must judge whether to sell out to the opponents, double or bid on.

### 1. Partscore decisions.

A good rule in making competitive decisions at the partscore level is:

> COMPETE TO THE *THREE LEVEL* IF YOU HAVE A FIT (ESPECIALLY A NINE-CARD OR LONGER FIT) AND YOUR SHARE OF THE HIGH CARDS. GO NO HIGHER WITHOUT *UNUSUALLY* GOOD DISTRIBUTION.

You may make an exception to this rule with bad trumps (there may be losers in your key suit); with values — particularly secondary values — in the opponents' suit, or with flat distribution. In any of those cases, you may *sell out* at the three level or even at the two level.

| South | West | North | East |
|-------|------|-------|------|
|       |      | 1 ♠   | 2 ♡  |
| 2 ♠   | 3 ♡  | Pass  | Pass |
| ?     |      |       |      |

**What should you, South, do with these hands?**

37. ♠ K 7 6 5
    ♡ 7 6 5
    ◇ K Q 6 5
    ♣ 7 6

Bid 3 ♠. You have four trumps, a decent hand and no values in the opponents' suit, so you can apply the rule.

38. ♠ J 9 5
    ♡ Q 7 6
    ◇ K Q 7 6
    ♣ 7 6 5

Pass. Your trumps are poor and you may have a spade trick or two to lose; your ♡Q is a potential defensive trick but is worth nothing on offense; your distribution is flat.

Both of these examples are clearcut. The problems come on the in-between hands.

| South | West | North | East |
|-------|------|-------|------|
| Pass | Pass | 1 ♣ | Pass |
| 1 ♡ | 1 ♠ | 2 ♣ | 2 ♠ |
| ? | | | |

39.  ♠ A 10 4 3
♡ Q 7 6 5 4
◇ 4 3
♣ Q 5

Bid 3 ♣. The Q-5 is adequate support for a suit partner rebid freely, and the ♠A will be a good card for partner. Perhaps you can beat them if they push to 3 ♠, but you should not sell out at the two level.

| South | West | North | East |
|-------|------|-------|------|
| | | Pass | 1 ♡ |
| 1 ♠ | 1 NT | 2 ♠ | 3 ◇ |
| ? | | | |

40.  ♠ A Q 9 4 3
♡ 6 5
◇ A 5
♣ A J 3 2

Pass. Your hand is defensive, and you will have to cope with a trump loser and the chance of a bad club split if you play 3 ♠.

| South | West | North | East |
|-------|------|-------|------|
| | | 1 ♠ | 2 ♡ |
| ? | | | |

41.  ♠ K 10 4
♡ A Q 9 3
◇ 7 6
♣ 8 7 6 5

Bid 2 ♠. It is usually wrong to double the opponents before you exhaust the possibilities of your own suit. Support partner for now.

## 2. When they sacrifice against your game.

You must decide whether to double and take what you can get against the save, or bid on. Do not *bid* directly over the save unless you are *certain* of making. When in doubt, you can always pass and see if partner has a firm opinion. *If you double* directly, you *suggest* that bidding on is unsafe. You do not promise to beat the opponents badly, you merely say you feel a plus score is more likely on defense:

| South | West | North | East |
|-------|------|-------|------|
|       |      | 1 ♡   | 2 ♣  |
| 2 ♡   | 3 ♣  | 4 ♡   | 5 ♣  |

You are vulnerable, the opponents are not. **What do you, South, call with these hands?**

42. ♠ K 6 5 3
    ♡ J 8 7
    ◇ Q 7 6 5
    ♣ 5 4

    Double. Your raise is so minimum that you do not want to pass and encourage partner to bid on.

43. ♠ A J 4 3
    ♡ K 6 5 4
    ◇ 6 5
    ♣ 6 5 4

    Pass. You have a sound raise with four trumps. Partner is probably short in clubs. If he wants to bid 5 ♡, fine.

Note that in both of these examples, partner's jump to 4 ♡ indicates that the hand *belongs* to your side. Therefore, you won't allow the opponents to play undoubled. Your side must do *something* at the five level.

| South | West | North | East |
|-------|------|-------|------|
| 1 ♡   | 2 ♣  | 2 ♡   | 3 ♣  |
| 4 ♡   | Pass | Pass  | 5 ♣  |
| ?     |      |       |      |

Only your side is vulnerable. **What do you, South, call with these hands?**

44. ♠ A Q 5
    ♡ A K J 7 5 3
    ◇ A 7 6
    ♣ 3

    Pass. This is *forcing*, and partner must act, since the opponents have clearly sacrificed. With a sound raise and no club values, partner may go on to 5 ♡. Otherwise, he will double.

45. ♠ A 5 4
    ♡ A K Q 5 4
    ◇ K J 7
    ♣ 6 5

    Double. You can't pass this one around since there was no assurance you could have made even 4 ♡. You could be off two club tricks for starters.

117

46. &spades; A K 6
&hearts; Q J 10 6 5
&diams; A K
&clubs; 7 6 5

Double. Be more anxious to double (at any level) when your defensive tricks lie in your short suits and will be more likely to cash.

Sometimes you can stampede the opponents into a sacrifice by bidding a confident-sounding game. Look at this situation:

| South | West | North | East |
|-------|------|-------|------|
|       | 1 ♠  | Double | 2 ♠ |
| ?     |      |       |      |

You are vulnerable, they are not. **What do you, South, call with this hand?**

47. &spades; 6 5 4
&hearts; A Q 9 4
&diams; 6 5
&clubs; K 9 6 4

Jump to 4♡! This is an overbid, but the opponents may be afraid to let you play it when they can play 4♠ not vulnerable. You can double that and expect to beat it.

Conversely, at times you may not want the opponents to sacrifice because their potential save appears to be a good one. Then you will have to bid tactically, jockeying for position.

| South | West | North | East |
|-------|------|-------|------|
|       |      | 1 ♠  | Pass |
| 2 ♡   | 4 ♣  | 4 ♡  | 5 ♣ |
| ?     |      |       |      |

You are vulnerable, they are not. **What do you, South, call with this hand?**

48. &spades; A K 10 4
&hearts; K J 8 5 4 2
&diams; 7 6 5
&clubs; —

Pass! You can probably make 6♡ or 6♠, maybe a grand slam; but the opponents surely have a good sacrifice at 7♣. Realistically, your aim should be to buy the contract at any level. Partner must act over 5♣, of course. If he doubles, you can pull to 5♡ or 6♡. If you give the impression of uncertainty, your chances of being left alone will improve. (On the deal on which this problem is based, you could make six of either major, but they would be down only 500 in 7♣. You would have done well to buy the contract at any level.)

### 3. Cooperative doubles.

You can extend the idea of doubling the opponents merely as a *suggestion*, especially if you can rely on partner to use his judgment instead of passing automatically.

| South | West | North | East |
|-------|------|-------|------|
|       | Pass | 1 ◇   | Pass |
| 1 ♡   | 2 ♣  | Pass  | Pass |
| ?     |      |       |      |

Neither side is vulnerable. **What do you, South, call with:**

49.   ♠ K Q 5 4     Double. This is cooperative, since you
      ♡ A 7 6 5      are underneath the 2 ♣ bidder, and any
      ◇ 7 6          trump honors you have are badly
      ♣ J 9 4        placed. Partner may have something in
clubs — perhaps he can pass for a substantial penalty. After all, he didn't raise hearts or rebid diamonds. If he has spades, he can bid them over your double.

| South | West | North | East |
|--------|------|-------|------|
|        | Pass | Pass  | 1 ♡  |
| Double | 1 ♠  | 2 ◇   | Pass |
| Pass   | 2 ♡  | Pass  | Pass |
| ?      |      |       |      |

Neither side is vulnerable. **What do you, South, do with:**

50.   ♠ A 10 6 5     Your best call is double. This suggests
      ♡ Q 5           a sound takeout double with good
      ◇ K 10 4       defensive values, no desire to raise
      ♣ A Q 10 4     diamonds and something in hearts. You
suggested heart shortness with your first double, so partner should not expect your hearts to be very strong. He can use his judgment.

# SUMMARY

Some basic principles provide a basis for good judgment in competitive bidding.

## I. BIDDING OVER A TAKEOUT DOUBLE

When partner's opening bid has been doubled for takeout, keep these ideas in mind.

---

1. Giving partner a clear description of your hand early in the auction may help him make a correct decision.
2. You have less reason to suggest a weak major suit as trumps (as you would do if your opponent had passed).
3. A redouble isn't always the best action even if you hold 10 or more HCP.

---

## II. MORE COMPETITIVE AUCTIONS

1. The *free bid principle* states that there must be a sound basis for an aggressive action taken when passing to partner is an option. This idea does *not* apply to raises, however.
2. You can pass an opponent's bid around to partner when you have no clear action. The *forcing pass* is a useful tool in competitive auctions.
3. When partner opens and right-hand opponent overcalls 1 NT, you will usually double for penalty with 9 or more HCP. Any other action denies the high-card strength to double, and all jump responses are preemptive.
4. When the opponents preempt, base any action on the assumption that partner holds 6 HCP or more. Strain to enter the auction when *you are very short in the preempter's suit.*
5. If an opponent opens 4 ♠, a *4 NT overcall* is used as a giant takeout double; a double is for penalty.

## III. YOUR COMPETITIVE JUDGMENT

1.  A rule of thumb to apply in making competitive *partscore* decisions:

> COMPETE TO THE THREE LEVEL IF YOU HAVE A FIT (ESPECIALLY A NINE-CARD OR LONGER FIT) AND YOUR SHARE OF THE HIGH CARDS. GO NO HIGHER WITHOUT *UNUSUALLY* GOOD DISTRIBUTION.

2.  When the opponents *sacrifice* against your game, do not bid on directly over the sacrifice unless you are sure of making — if in doubt, *pass* to partner and hear his opinion. If you *double* you do not promise to beat the opponents a lot; you only want to *discourage partner from bidding further.*)

## TEST YOUR COMPREHENSION OF THE MATERIAL IN THIS CHAPTER: BIDDING OVER A TAKEOUT DOUBLE

Partner opens 1♣, right-hand opponent doubles. Neither side is vulnerable. What do you say with these hands?

1.  ♠ K 6 5
    ♡ 6 5
    ◇ A 7 6 5
    ♣ 8 7 6 4

2.  ♠ A J 7
    ♡ A 5
    ◇ 8 7 6 5
    ♣ 8 7 6 5

3.  ♠ Q J 8 7
    ♡ 3
    ◇ 8 7 5
    ♣ J 7 6 5 3

4.  ♠ Q 10 5 4 3
    ♡ —
    ◇ Q J 8 7 6
    ♣ 5 4 3

5.  ♠ 7 6
    ♡ Q 10 6 5
    ◇ K 9 8
    ♣ K 6 5 4

6.  ♠ 8
    ♡ J 7 6 5 4
    ◇ K 8 7
    ♣ A 9 6 5

7. &spades; 6 5
&hearts; A Q 6 5
&diams; K 7
&clubs; Q J 7 6 5

8. &spades; A K 6 3
&hearts; 5 4
&diams; A 7 6
&clubs; J 7 6 5

9. &spades; 8
&hearts; A J 8 7
&diams; K Q 8 7
&clubs; Q 9 8 7

10. &spades; 5 4
&hearts; 8 7 6
&diams; A 7
&clubs; K Q 10 8 7 6

11. &spades; K 5 4 3
&hearts; 9
&diams; A Q 8 7
&clubs; 8 7 6 5

12. &spades; 6 5
&hearts; 5
&diams; J 7 6
&clubs; K J 10 7 6 5 4

Partner opens 1 &diams; , RHO doubles. Neither side is vulnerable. What do you say with these hands?

1. &spades; 5 4
&hearts; A 5 4
&diams; K 7 6 5 4
&clubs; 7 6 5

2. &spades; 5
&hearts; A 7 6
&diams; J 9 8 7 5
&clubs; 8 7 6 5

3. &spades; K 8 7
&hearts; Q 6 5
&diams; 7 6 5
&clubs; K 9 8 7

4. &spades; K 7 6
&hearts; Q 8 7 6
&diams; 7 6 5
&clubs; K 7 6

5. &spades; K Q 9 8 7
&hearts; 6 5
&diams; K 6 5
&clubs; 7 6 5

6. &spades; A 6
&hearts; K Q 6 5
&diams; 6 5
&clubs; Q 7 6 5 4

7. &spades; A 4
&hearts; 5 4
&diams; K Q 6 5 4
&clubs; A 6 5 4

8. &spades; K Q 10 6 5
&hearts; A 6 5
&diams; K 6 5
&clubs; 4 3

# QUIZ ON COMPETITIVE AUCTIONS

1.  You open 1♣, partner responds 1♥, RHO overcalls 1♠. What do you say with:

    a.  ♠ Q 6 5
        ♥ J 8
        ◇ K 6 5 4
        ♣ A Q J 5

    b.  ♠ A J 7
        ♥ K 8
        ◇ 7 6 5 3
        ♣ A Q J 3

    c.  ♠ A 4 3
        ♥ K 7 6 5
        ◇ 5 4
        ♣ A J 7 6

    d.  ♠ A 3
        ♥ K 7 6
        ◇ 7 6 5
        ♣ A J 7 6 5

2.  You open 1♥, partner responds 3♥ (forcing). RHO overcalls 3♠. What do you say with:

    a.  ♠ 5 4
        ♥ A Q 7 6 5
        ◇ K J 2
        ♣ A 3 2

3.  Partner opens 1♥, RHO overcalls 1 NT. Neither side vulnerable. What do you say with:

    a.  ♠ K Q 10 6 5
        ♥ 5 4
        ◇ A 5 4
        ♣ 5 4 3

    b.  ♠ 7 6 5
        ♥ A 6 5
        ◇ 7 6
        ♣ A Q 6 5 4

    c.  ♠ 6 5
        ♥ J 8 7 6
        ◇ A Q 6 5
        ♣ 4 3 2

    d.  ♠ 8
        ♥ J 9 8 6 4
        ◇ Q 8 7 6 5
        ♣ 5 4

    e.  ♠ 6 5
        ♥ 6 5
        ◇ K Q 10 9 7 6
        ♣ J 7 6

    f.  ♠ 5
        ♥ 5 4
        ◇ J 6 5
        ♣ K J 10 7 6 5 4

4. Neither side vulnerable. RHO deals and opens 3 ◊. What do you say with:

a.  ♠ A K 4 3        b.  ♠ 5 4
    ♡ K J 6 5            ♡ A K Q 4 3
    ◊ 4 3               ◊ A 3
    ♣ A J 6             ♣ Q 7 6 5

c.  ♠ 4 3            d.  ♠ Q 6
    ♡ A Q 4             ♡ A 5 4
    ◊ A Q 10 5          ◊ K 6
    ♣ Q 6 5 4           ♣ A K Q 6 5 4

e.  ♠ A K 6
    ♡ A Q 6
    ◊ K 7 6
    ♣ A 6 5 4

## QUIZ ON COMPETITIVE JUDGMENT

1.
| South | West | North | East |
|-------|------|-------|------|
|       |      | 1 ♡   | 2 ♣  |
| 2 ♡   | 3 ♣  | Pass  | Pass |
| ?     |      |       |      |

What do you, South, do with these hands?

a.  ♠ 4             b.  ♠ K 9 5
    ♡ A 6 5             ♡ J 6 5
    ◊ Q 10 7 6 5 4      ◊ Q 8 7 5
    ♣ 7 6 5             ♣ Q 7 6

| 2. | South | West | North | East |
|----|-------|------|-------|------|
|    |       |      | 1 ♠   | 2 ◇  |
|    | 2 ♣   | 3 ◇  | 4 ♠   | 5 ◇  |
|    | ?     |      |       |      |

Your side is vulnerable, the opponents are not. What do you, South, do with these hands?

a.　♠ J 7 6 5　　　　b.　♠ K 10 5 4
　　♡ Q 10 6 5　　　　　♡ A J 7 5
　　◇ K 6　　　　　　　　◇ 8 7 6
　　♣ 7 6 5　　　　　　　♣ 7 6

| 3. | South | West | North | East |
|----|-------|------|-------|------|
|    | 1 ♡   | 1 ♠  | 2 ♡   | 2 ♠  |
|    | 4 ♡   | Pass | Pass  | 4 ♠  |
|    | ?     |      |       |      |

Your side is vulnerable, the opponents are not. What do you, South, do with these hands?

a.　♠ 4　　　　　　　　b.　♠ A 6
　　♡ A K J 7 6 5　　　　♡ A K 7 6 5
　　◇ A Q 8　　　　　　　◇ K J 6 5
　　♣ A 10 6　　　　　　　♣ Q 4

| 4. | South | West | North | East |
|----|-------|------|-------|------|
|    | Pass  | Pass | 1 ♡   | Pass |
|    | 1 ♠   | 2 ◇  | Pass  | Pass |
|    | ?     |      |       |      |

Both sides are vulnerable. What do you, South, do with:

a.　♠ A J 6 5 4
　　♡ 8
　　◇ K 7 4
　　♣ Q 9 5 3

## SOLUTIONS TO QUIZ ON BIDDING OVER A TAKEOUT DOUBLE

1. 2♠
2. Pass, support spades later.
3. 3♠, preemptive
4. 4♠
5. 1 NT
6. Pass
7. Redouble
8. Redouble
9. Pass, then double whatever they bid.
10. 2♣
11. 2 NT, *Jordan.*
12. 3♣, preemptive

1. 2◊
2. 3◊
3. 1 NT
4. 1 NT
5. 1♠
6. Redouble
7. Redouble
8. Redouble

# SOLUTIONS TO QUIZ ON COMPETITIVE AUCTIONS

1.  a   Pass.   Not enough for a free bid of 1 NT.
    b   1 NT
    c   2♡
    d   2♡
2.  a   Pass   (forcing). Partner may be happy to double. If not, he can always bid 4♡.
3.  a   Double
    b   Double
    c   2♡
    d   3♡,   preemptive
    e   2◇
    f   3♣,   preemptive
4.  a   Double
    b   3♡
    c   Pass
    d   3 NT
    e   Double , bid 3 NT if partner responds in a major.

## SOLUTIONS TO QUIZ ON COMPETITIVE JUDGMENT

1.  a   3♡
    b   Pass
2.  a   Double
    b   Pass. You can encourage partner to bid 5♠ with your sound raise.
3.  a   Pass. You have no clear action, so let partner decide.
    b   Double
4.  a   Double .This is cooperative, since you sit underneath West's diamonds. Partner may have something in diamonds (he did not raise spades or rebid hearts), and he may be able to pass for penalty.

# Chapter 8

## FINE POINTS OF DECLARER PLAY: DECEPTION AND PSYCHOLOGY

Earlier, we saw that good *technique* is one mark of a capable declarer. There are, however, equally important aspects of declarer play — the practice of DECEPTION and the application of PSYCHOLOGY.

On many hands you declare, even perfect technique won't help — the contract will always be defeated if the opponents defend perfectly. Your objective must be to induce them to err.

Deceptive play on defense can backfire because you may fool your partner as well as (or instead of) declarer. On defense, therefore, you must wait for the right moment for deception. As declarer, though, you have no partner to harm, so you can safely indulge in all kinds of trickery. For example, as declarer you may:

1. Falsecard at will.
2. Discard deceptively.
3. Win a trick with a card that leaves the defenders in doubt about your holding. Often, you win a trick with a *high* card when a lower one would do.
4. Refuse to win a trick to create a false impression of weakness.

Most of the situations we will look at are common. Memorize them so you can produce a good deceptive play when the opportunity comes along. Good timing may be required to make the deception work.

1.
       ♠ A Q 2
       ♡ J 9 5 3
       ◊ K Q 2
       ♣ J 8 5

       ♠ K 6
       ♡ Q 10 8 7 6 4
       ◊ A 7 6
       ♣ Q 6

You, South, are declarer in 4 ♡. West leads the ♣A (suggesting the king). This may be the best-known position of all. Declarer should play his ♣Q. West may be persuaded not to cash his second club, in which case declarer will take a discard on dummy's third spade.

2.
       ♠ Q 10
       ♡ 5 4
       ◊ J 10 5 3
       ♣ A Q J 7 5

       ♠ 7 5
       ♡ A Q 2
       ◊ A Q 9 6 4
       ♣ K 8 4

You, South, are declarer in 3 NT. The opening lead is a low heart, East playing the jack. **How should you play?**

If the diamond finesse works, you will make overtricks. If not, the probable spade switch will set you. To induce the opponents not to shift to spades, you win the first trick with the ♡A, not the queen. West will naturally place his partner with the ♡Q. Then you lead your ♣8 to dummy's jack. (It is unethical to consciously try to convey the impression that you are taking a finesse, but neither must you play as though you clearly expect the jack to win.) Finesse the ◊J. If West wins the king, he will probably play a second heart, expecting to run the heart suit. Note that if you win the first trick with your ♡Q, West will probably find the spade switch in desperation.

3.
    ♠ 9 4 3
    ♡ 5
    ◇ A 9 8 5
    ♣ J 9 6 4 2

    ♠ Q 6
    ♡ K J 4 2
    ◇ K 6 4
    ♣ A Q 10 5

You, South, are declarer in 1 NT. The opening lead is the ♡ 7, and East puts on the ten. **How do you play?**

This is the same idea. Winning with a higher card than necessary may have strange effects. Win the ♡ K! West will credit his partner with the jack. Next, you go to the ◇ A and pass the ♣ 9. If West wins, he will cash his ♡ A and ♡ Q (or underlead them again), expecting to run the suit. The dreaded spade shift is unlikely.

4.
    ♠ J 10 9
    ♡ 5 4
    ◇ A Q 10 9 4
    ♣ J 10 6

    ♠ A Q 7
    ♡ J 9 2
    ◇ K J 5
    ♣ A Q 9 4

You, South opened 1 NT and become declarer in 3 NT. West leads the ♠ 5, and East plays low on dummy's jack. **How do you play?**

Overtake the jack with your queen, hoping to create the impression that you started with A-Q doubleton. Lead the ◇ J to the queen and take the club finesse. If it loses, West may underlead his ♠ K again.

5.
&spades; J 8 5 4
&hearts; K Q 4
&diams; K 7 4
&clubs; 9 3 2

&spades; A K Q 7
&hearts; J 8 3
&diams; A Q 3
&clubs; Q 8 4

You, South, are declarer in 4 &spades;. West leads the &clubs; A (suggesting the king as well), and East plays the five. **What card should declarer play?**

The *eight* is correct. By concealing the &clubs; 4, declarer hopes to make East's five look like an encouraging signal. If West continues with the &clubs; A, an impossible game will likely come in.

6.
&spades; A K J
&hearts; J 6 5
&diams; J 9 3
&clubs; K 7 6 3

&spades; Q 8 4 2
&hearts; 10 7
&diams; A Q 10 7
&clubs; A J 2

You, South, are declarer in 3 NT. The opening lead is the &spades; 10. You would like West to lead another spade if the diamond finesse loses, so you should try to make a continuation attractive. Win the &spades; K at trick one. East plays the six, and your drop your *eight*. Again, West may misinterpret his partner's signal because you conceal your lower spots.

7.

     ♠ K Q 6 5
     ♡ J 6 4
     ◇ J 8
     ♣ A 5 4 3

     ♠ A 7 2
     ♡ A 9
     ◇ Q 10 7 3 2
     ♣ K Q 7

You, South, are declarer in 3 NT. The opening lead is the ◇ 4, won by East's ace. **What card should declarer play?**

The *seven,* concealing the two and three. Declarer wants East to think that West led from a *six*-card suit, so East will continue diamonds instead of shifting to hearts.

8.

     ♠ J 8 7 5
     ♡ Q 7 6 2
     ◇ K 3
     ♣ A K 8

     ♠ A K Q 9 2
     ♡ 10 8 3
     ◇ Q 9 2
     ♣ 4 3

You, South, reach 4 ♠ after West opened 1 ♡. The opening lead is the ♡ A, East playing the four. **What card should declarer play?**

Play the *three* quickly. This is no time to be cute. If you play the eight or ten, West may interpret East's four as the start of an echo and continue. The four is surely a singleton, but if you play your three, West may think *you* have the singleton and switch.

## 9. What card would you play in this situation?

$\heartsuit$ K 7 4 2

$\heartsuit$ J 10 9

You, South, are declarer in a spade contract, reached after East opened 1 $\heartsuit$. West leads the $\heartsuit$ 3 to East's queen.

You must play the *ten*. East may place his partner with J-9-3. If you play the nine or jack, East will work out the position. West would lead the 10 from 10-9-3, the jack from J-10-3.

10.
      $\spadesuit$ 7 5 4
      $\heartsuit$ Q 6 5
      $\diamond$ K 7 6
      $\clubsuit$ K 4 3 2

      $\spadesuit$ K Q 3
      $\heartsuit$ J 7
      $\diamond$ A J 10 5
      $\clubsuit$ A Q J 6

You, South, are declarer in 3 NT. The opening lead is a low spade. East plays the jack. **Which card should declarer play?**

Win the $\spadesuit$ *K*. You want West to think his partner may have the $\spadesuit$ Q. You will take a diamond finesse into West's hand. If it loses, you would like him to lead another spade. However . . .

11.
      $\spadesuit$ 7 5 4
      $\heartsuit$ Q 6 5
      $\diamond$ K 7 6
      $\clubsuit$ K 4 3 2

      $\spadesuit$ K Q
      $\heartsuit$ A 7 2
      $\diamond$ A J 10 5 3
      $\clubsuit$ A 7 6

Here, you win the $\spadesuit$ *Q*. You *want* West to know you have the king. Perhaps he won't lay down the $\spadesuit$ A if he gets in with the $\diamond$ Q.

133

12.                    ♠ 7 5 3

                       ♣ A K 10

West leads the ♣2 against your notrump contract, and East plays the queen. Win the *ace,* leaving both defenders in doubt about the location of the king.

13.                    ♠ 7 5 4

                       ♣ A K Q

West has led the ♣J against your notrump contract. **What card should win the trick?**

Be honest and win the *queen, the card you are known to hold from the lead.* If you win the ace, East will know you have the king as well as the queen. Look at this deal.

14.                    ♠ Q 7 4
                       ♡ A 5 4 3
                       ◇ 7 6
                       ♣ A J 10 5

    ♠ A 9                              ♠ 10 8 6 5 3
    ♡ K J 9 6          N               ♡ Q 7
    ◇ J 10 9 5 2    W     E            ◇ 8 4 3
    ♣ 6 2              S               ♣ K 8 4

                       ♠ K J 2
                       ♡ 10 8 2
                       ◇ A K Q
                       ♣ Q 9 7 3

South, declarer in 3 NT, won the opening ◇J lead with his ace and ran the ♣9 to East's king. East knew the diamond situation, so he switched to the ♡Q, and declarer went down one. Note that if declarer wins the first trick with the ◇Q, East will surely return a diamond, playing partner for A-J-10-x-x or K-J-10-x-x.

15.          ♠ A 6
                 ♡ K 8 6 5 3
                 ◊ J 7 6
                 ♣ A K 4

                 ♠ 9 4
                 ♡ A 4
                 ◊ K 10 4 2
                 ♣ Q J 7 6 5

You, South, are declarer in 3 NT. The opening lead is the ♠ 5.
**How do you play?**

Win the first trick, disdaining a hold-up that would probably help
the defenders judge the position. Then lead the ◊ J from dummy,
intending to go up with your king if East plays low. If East has the
ace, perhaps he will duck, thinking that you are about to lose a finesse
to West's queen.

16.          ♠ J 7 6
                 ♡ K 9 4
                 ◊ 6 5 4
                 ♣ A K J 5

                 ♠ K 2
                 ♡ A Q 10 7 5 3
                 ◊ A K 3
                 ♣ Q 8

| *South* | *West* | *North* | *East* |
|---------|--------|---------|--------|
|         |        |         | 3 ♠    |
| 4 ♡     | Pass   | 5 ♡     | Pass   |
| 6 ♡     | (All Pass) |     |        |

West leads the ♠ 3. **How do you play?**

The opening lead is an obvious singleton, so you will be down
if East wins the ♠ A and returns a spade. But suppose you drop your
♠ K under the ace! This looks odd, but you have nothing to lose.
If East places his partner with the doubleton spade, he may switch
to a diamond.

17.

♠ 6 5
♡ A 10 4
◇ A J 10 4
♣ J 8 4 3

♠ J 10 9
♡ Q 7
◇ K Q 7 5
♣ A K 10 5

You, South, are declarer in 3 NT. The opening lead is the ♣ 6, and dummy's eight wins the first trick. **What do you do next?**

There are eight top tricks, but no strong prospects for a ninth. If you make a heart play, the opponents will surely switch to spades upon winning. Perhaps the best strategy is to lead spades yourself, masking your weakness. Defenders sometimes have a mental block about leading a suit that declarer seems to like. So you play a spade to your nine at trick two, and West wins. Look at the problem from his point of view. His hand could be:

♠ A Q 4
♡ K J 3
◇ 9 3 2
♣ Q 9 7 6

Another club lead may cost, a diamond looks dangerous, and your spade lead has thrown up a smokescreen around that suit. West may switch to a heart, hoping to find partner with the queen.

18.          K 4 3 2

             Q 5

Suppose you are declarer in a spade contract, and you need two tricks from this side suit. Of course, you start by leading low from dummy to your queen. As you were hoping, it holds. Now you could lead low toward dummy and duck, and duck another round later, hoping the ace will fall, but a deceptive play may give East a headache. Go back to dummy and lead low toward your five! If East has A-10-x-x, he must guess whether to play his ace or play low again.

136

Note that many of these deceptive plays require imaginative defenders. Your beautiful deceptive plays will be wasted on a poor opponent. Save them for someone who can appreciate them.

---

No discussion of psychology in declarer play would be complete without a mention of *table presence* or *table "feel."* The reputations of several famous experts rest in part on their ability to *sense* everything that goes on at the table.

What we collectively called table presence actually has several aspects.

1. The ability to draw conclusions from extraneous events, such as the opponents' hesitations, mannerisms and remarks. (However, it is unethical to act on unauthorized information available from similar actions by your partner.)
2. The ability to look into your opponent's mind and anticipate what he will do.
3. The ability to sense an opportunity and apply good technique to take advantage.

The first area is the one most often associated with the term *table presence.*

19.
  ♠ Q 9 4 2
  ♡ K 10 4
  ◊ K 4 3
  ♣ A Q 7

  ♠ A K 8 6 3
  ♡ A J 2
  ◊ 7 2
  ♣ J 10 4

You, South, are declarer in 4 ♠. The opening lead is the ◊ J, which wins. Another diamond goes to East's queen, and you ruff the ◊ A. You play three rounds of trumps, ending in hand (East had J-10-x, West throws two diamonds), and you finesse the ♣ J, losing to East's king. A club is returned to dummy. On the next club West shows out, discarding a heart. **How should you play the hearts?**

East is known to have had five clubs, three spades and three diamonds; therefore, two hearts. The odds are 5-to-2 that *West* has any one of the missing hearts. Also, East might have opened the bidding with:

♠ J 10 x
♡ Q x
◇ A Q x
♣ K x x x x

Take your heart finesse through West.

Now suppose *East was dealer and paused for some time before passing.* You judge that East actually had a problem with his hand (and wasn't merely daydreaming). Would East have anything to think about with:

♠ J 10 x
♡ x x
◇ A Q x
♣ K x x x x

No, he would pass quickly. But with the ♡Q in addition, East might be tempted to open. He might consider the matter for a few seconds. This kind of hand sometimes produces a *12-point twitch* in less experienced players.

Remember the advice I offered on percentage play. Use mathematics as a guide only when there is nothing else to go on.

In case you are wondering, it is perfectly okay to draw an inference from your opponent's hesitation, as on the deal above. However, such inferences are drawn *at your own risk*. If East was thinking about where to take his wife for dinner, you have no recourse. You can get redress (in tournament bridge) only when there is a *deliberate* attempt to deceive you.

20.

♠ A K 4
♡ 8 6
♦ 8 7 6 5 3
♣ A 10 4

♠ 8 5 2
♡ A 9
♦ A K 2
♣ K J 9 8 5

You, South, are declarer in 3 NT. The opening lead is a heart, driving out your ace, and you must guess clubs to make the contract. It costs nothing to lead your ♣J to observe West's reaction. A veteran West would play low smoothly regardless of his holding. If West is inexperienced, he may cover the jack, or hesitate and give his holding away. If West fumbles for a card and plays low, it is possible he does *not* have the queen. If a player of moderate skill holds the queen, he is likely to be anxious to play low smoothly.

*Timing* is a factor in playing this card combination. It is best to lead your ♣J as soon as you can, before the defenders can assess dummy and picture your probable club holding. Of course, it is unsporting to *slam* down your ♣J a split second after winning the first trick and expect West to maintain a high standard of ethics.

If the cards are as follows, you have another gambit available:

21.

♠ A K 4
♡ 8 6
♦ 8 7 6 5 3
♣ A 10 4

♠ Q J 10
♡ A 9
♦ A K 2
♣ K J 9 8 5

**How do you play after a heart lead, won by your ace?**

Lead the ♠J at trick two and see how West reacts when he does *not* have the queen! You can win the spade in dummy, come back to a diamond honor and lead your ♣J. Perhaps you will see a different reaction that may suggest the winning play.

139

# SUMMARY

On some hands, declarer cannot profit from flawless technique because the contract will be defeated with competent defense. Declarer's aim must be to induce the defenders to err, and the emphasis shifts from technique to guile.

Because declarer has no partner to worry about, he can indulge in all sorts of trickery. For instance, he may:

1. Falsecard at will.
2. Discard deceptively.
3. Win a trick with a card that leaves the defenders in the dark about his holding. Often, declarer wins with a high card when a lower one would do.
4. Refuse to win a trick to create a false impression of weakness.

In considering deceptive play by declarer, keep these points in mind:

1. Many deceptive plays are standard, and the positions should be memorized.
2. *Timing* is a factor in executing most deceptive plays. A long pause beforehand will render the deception ineffective.
3. Many deceptive plays require good defenders with enough imagination to fall for them. Don't waste a beautiful deceptive play on an opponent who can't visualize the problem you create for him.

The psychological aspects of declarer play include *table presence* or *table feel* — the term usually denotes the ability to draw conclusions from extraneous events, such as opponents' hesitations, remarks and mannerisms. (It is unethical, however, to act on information available from *partner's* actions.)

# TEST YOUR COMPREHENSION OF THE MATERIAL IN THIS CHAPTER:

## QUIZ ON DECEPTION

1.
♠ J 10 3
♡ 4 3 2
◇ A K 9 5
♣ J 10 4

♠ A K 7
♡ J 8 5
◇ Q J 10
♣ A Q 9 5

You are declarer in 3 NT. West leads the ♠6. Plan the play.

2.
♠ 10 3
♡ 8 7 5
◇ Q 8 7 4 2
♣ 7 4 2

♠ A K Q 6
♡ A K Q
◇ 9 6 5 3
♣ A K

You are declarer in 3 NT. West leads the ♣Q. Plan the play.

3.
♠ Q 4
♡ A 6
◇ J 10 6 5 3
♣ 7 5 4 3

♠ K 10 9 8 5 3
♡ 7 3
◇ A K
♣ K Q J

You are declarer in 4♠. West leads the ♡K. Plan the play.

4.                  ♠ Q 6 4
                    ♡ 5
                    ◊ A Q J 10 5
                    ♣ 8 6 5 4

                  ♠ A
                  ♡ A K Q J 9 8 6 4
                  ◊ 9 4
                  ♣ K Q

You are declarer in 6♡. West leads the ♠J. Plan the play.

5.                  ♠ Q 7 3
                  ♡ J 9 4
                  ◊ 9 6 5 3
                  ♣ 8 6 4

                  ♠ 5 2
                  ♡ A K Q 10 7 3
                  ◊ A 8
                  ♣ A Q J

You are declarer in 4♡. West leads the ♠A (suggesting the king as well). East plays the ♠6. Which card do you play?

6.                  ♠ Q 7 5
                  ♡ K 4
                  ◊ 8 6 5 4 2
                  ♣ A K 4

                  ♠ —
                  ♡ A Q J 9 8 7 6 3
                  ◊ K Q 7
                  ♣ Q 6

You are declarer in 6♡. West leads the ◊3. Plan the play.

7.

     ♠ A 7
     ♡ 8 6 5 3
     ◊ K 5 3
     ♣ K 7 5 3

     ♠ J 4
     ♡ K Q 4
     ◊ A Q 6 4 2
     ♣ A 8 2

You are declarer in 3 NT. (You opened 1 NT, North raised to 3 NT.) West leads the ◊ J, East plays the eight. Plan the play.

8.

     ♠ A 7 5
     ♡ A 4
     ◊ K J 6 4
     ♣ 10 8 4 3

     ♠ K 8 4
     ♡ J 7 3
     ◊ Q 10 5 3
     ♣ A K 6

You are declarer in 3 NT. West leads the ♣2, East plays the queen. Plan the play.

9.

     ♠ Q 7 5
     ♡ J 6 4
     ◊ K 10 6 5
     ♣ J 5 4

     ♠ A 4
     ♡ A 8 5 3
     ◊ A Q J 4
     ♣ A Q 7

You are declarer in 3 NT. West leads the ♡K, and you win the ace. How do you continue?

143

1.
       ♠ Q 9 4 2
       ♡ K 10 7
       ◇ K 6 4
       ♣ A Q 3

       ♠ A K 7 6 3
       ♡ A J 6
       ◇ 5 3
       ♣ J 8 4

You are declarer in 4 ♠. East passed as dealer, but only after some thought. West leads the ◇ J and continues a diamond to East's queen. You ruff East's ◇ A and draw trumps, finding that East had J-10-5. A club finesse loses to East's king, and a club is returned. How do you play the hearts?

2.
       ♠ K 6 4
       ♡ A K 4
       ◇ Q J 2
       ♣ A Q 6 2

       ♠ A J 3
       ♡ J 10 7 3
       ◇ A 10 9 4
       ♣ K 7

You are declarer in 6 NT. West leads a low spade and looks unhappy when you win the jack. You lead a heart to dummy and try the diamond finesse, which loses to West. A heart is returned. How do you play?

3. ♠ Q 5
  ♡ A K 5
  ◇ A 10 4
  ♣ 8 7 6 5 3

  ♠ A 8
  ♡ Q J 10
  ◇ K J 9 8 3
  ♣ A K 2

You are declarer in 3 NT. West leads a low spade, and dummy's queen is covered by the king. Plan the play.

## SOLUTIONS TO QUIZ ON DECEPTION

1. Play the ♠ J from dummy and *overtake* it with the king if East plays low. If the club finesse loses to West, you hope that he will continue spades instead of shifting to a heart.
2. Win the club and lead a *low spade* toward the ten, hoping to sneak it by. This is your best chance.
3. Win and return a heart. If the opponents think you need to ruff hearts in dummy, they may break the trump suit for you.
4. Play the ♣ Q from dummy. If the king covers and your ace wins, you create a powerful suggestion that you have another spade. If the diamond finesse loses, East may continue spades. (Take the diamond finesse right away to prevent East from discarding a high club as you draw trumps.)
5. Play the ♠ 5, hoping to make East's six look like an encouraging signal. If West continues with the ♠ K, you will discard your diamond loser on the ♠ Q.
6. When East wins the ◇ A, drop your *king*. The diamond lead is probably a singleton, but perhaps you can talk East into trying to cash the ♠ A instead of returning a diamond.
7. *Duck* the first trick, following with the six from hand. West probably has J-10-9-7. If he continues the suit, you have gained some valuable time.
8. Win the ♣ A and return a low club toward dummy. West will be tempted to duck with his J-9-x-x, afraid that his partner has the doubleton K-Q. If you steal a club trick, you can shift to diamonds for nine tricks.

9. Lead a *low* club from hand. If East wins, he can do nothing to hurt you. If West has the ♣K, he probably will duck, saving a trick (he thinks) with K-10-x-x or K-10-x. If the ♣J holds, you can return to hand and lead toward the ♡J for your ninth trick. Note that if you lead a heart back at trick two, West may win and hurt you with a spade shift through dummy.

## SOLUTIONS TO QUIZ ON TABLE PRESENCE

1. East has shown 10 HCP in the play so far and seems to have had a balanced hand. With the ♡Q in addition, he might have been tempted to open the bidding, which would account for his huddle. Play your ♡K and return a heart towards your jack.
2. West has already lost one trick by leading from the ♠Q, so East surely has the ♡Q. Play the other high heart from dummy. If the queen doesn't drop, maybe East can be squeezed in hearts and clubs.
3. The problem is to locate the ◇Q. You could lead the ◇J to see West's reaction, but first lead the ♡J and see how West reacts when he does *not* have a queen. Win the ace in dummy, return to your ♣A and lead the ◇J. You may notice a different reaction that will help you make a winning decision.

# Chapter 9

## INTRODUCTION TO MATCHPOINT STRATEGY

DUPLICATE BRIDGE is the type of bridge played in all the big national and international tournaments. In addition, there are local duplicate bridge clubs in every fair-sized city, and the game may even be enjoyed at home. The game is called *duplicate* because every hand is played more than once (but by different players) under conditions that are exactly duplicated — same cards in each hand, same dealer and vulnerability. This allows for a *comparison of results* when the game ends. The winners are the players who *made the most* of the cards they were dealt on each hand. It is possible to lose 1700 points on a hand and still get the best score of any player who held your cards — it could happen that the opposing players bid and made a grand slam at all the other tables. Skill at the game, not the luck of the deal, becomes the primary factor in determining a winner, making duplicate a stimulating form of competition.

*AT MATCHPOINTS, YOU WILL FREQUENTLY FACE DIFFICULT BIDDING DECISIONS.*

## SCORING

Scoring at duplicate is similar to the style used in *Chicago* or four-deal bridge. Every deal is scored as a separate entity. There are no rubbers, nor are partscores carried over from one deal to the next. Instead, an arbitrary bonus is awarded for making a game or part-score — this bonus is added to the trick score.

| | |
|---|---|
| For making a vulnerable game | 500 |
| For making a non-vulnerable game | 300 |
| For making a partscore | 50 |

The dealer and vulnerability for each deal, or *board*, are pre-set. Honors are not counted. Penalty points and bonuses for slams are mostly unchanged from rubber bridge. However, the penalty for doubled undertricks not vulnerable increases by 300 points after the third undertrick, and the bonus for making a redoubled contract is 100 points instead of 50. These changes were instituted in the latest (1987) edition of the *Laws of Duplicate Contract Bridge*.

If, therefore, your side plays a vulnerable 4 ♠ and makes five, your score is 650. If you play 3 ◊ and make four, you score 130. Note that the score for overtricks is lumped in with the score for tricks bid and made.

### MATCHPOINT DUPLICATE

There are several forms of duplicate competition. The best is probably the *knockout teams,* where two teams of four players play a long match of boards head-to-head, with the winners advancing to the next round. However, the most common form of duplicate, and the one with which most players first come in contact, is *matchpoints*.

This is the basic form of the game. Each board is played from three to 13 times (depending on the number of competing pairs) with the usual comparison of results. In the comparison, your pair scores *one matchpoint* for every result you *beat* on each deal, and *one-half matchpoint* for every result you *tie*. The pair with the most matchpoints over the entire set of deals (anywhere from 21 to 28) is the winner.

It is important to remember that the *margin* by which you outscore your competitors (who, in reality, are the players who hold your cards

148

when the deal is replayed) is unimportant — *just 10 points is enough.* Your fate is determined by *how many* of your competitors you outscore by *any* margin (or tie). This idea profoundly affects the strategy of the game. Every pair tries hard to get the most from each deal in an effort to get that small, but possibly crucial, edge over the competitors. Strategy at duplicate is strikingly different in many respects from good rubber-bridge strategy.

## I. CONSTRUCTIVE BIDDING

When your side has most of the high cards, you are the master of your fate. You must make the most of your chances for a good matchpoint score. Therefore, prefer to play in *notrump* or in a *major* suit, especially at the game level (when most of the pairs holding your cards will earn some plus score), even if it means taking a risk. Look at this hand:

♠ 3 2
♡ K Q 3
◇ A J 10 5
♣ A 10 3 2

♠ A K
♡ J 4 2
◇ K 6 4
♣ K J 8 6 4

You, South, open 1 ♣ and hear a (forcing) raise to 3 ♣. At rubber bridge you might think fleetingly of 5 ♣, but at matchpoints you must bid 3 NT. Quite often, you will make four or five, scoring 430 or 460 (not vulnerable). If 5 ♣ yields 400 or 420, you would lose matchpoints to the pairs in 3 NT and could get a bottom score.

Note that 5 ♣ is cold on these cards (if clubs do not split, declarer can strip the major suits and endplay an opponent with his trump trick) whereas 3 NT may go down (a spade is led, the ♣Q doesn't fall, and declarer misguesses in diamonds). Nevertheless, 3 NT is the correct contract in a matchpoint event because it offers the chances for the *largest plus score,* the one most likely to be a *top* (the best matchpoint score on the deal).

149

♠ Q 5
♡ J 6 5 4
◇ A 8 7 6
♣ J 9 8

Your partner opens 1♠, you respond 1 NT, he rebids 2◇. At rubber bridge you would pass. You're in a safe contract that rates to make. At matchpoints you take a *false preference* to 2♠, straining to play in the major suit opposite an almost-certain five-card suit. You may be in a riskier contract (and may go down more often), but the rewards are greater — and that's the name of the game.

♠ K J 4
♡ J 5 4 3
◇ 5 4
♣ A 7 6 5

Partner opens 1♣, you respond 1♡, he rebids 1♠. At rubber bridge you take a club preference. At matchpoints raise to 2♠ (or pass, if very conservative).

♠ J 9 6 5 3
♡ 6 5
◇ A 7 6 4
♣ J 3

Partner opens 1◇, you respond 1♠, he rebids 2♣. Bid 2◇. You must draw the line somewhere, and a 2♠ rebid would be going too far. Partner could have a singleton spade, and besides, your hand is so bad that *any* plus score may be okay in the matchpoint column. You don't need to assume that a big plus will be needed to outscore the other pairs.

♠ J 6
♡ K 10 6 5
◇ Q 9 5
♣ A 8 5 3

After three passes your partner opens 1♠. At rubber bridge, where the main objective is bidding games, you might respond with a mildly encouraging 2♣. At matchpoints a 1 NT response is better. Playing in a good partial can earn a high matchpoint score as easily as bidding a good game, and 1 NT is often a *good matchpoint contract.* There is some chance that partner opened a light hand in fourth seat, hoping for a plus. If you bid 2♣, you may punish him for his enterprise.

At rubber bridge you are rewarded with a bonus if you bid and make game (or slam), so your bidding is often aggressive in an effort to reach game. But at matchpoints your objective is not to bid a game but to outscore the other pairs. You might try a game at rubber bridge, especially when vulnerable, with a 40% chance of making it — you have more to gain than you have to lose. At matchpoints, though, you should seldom bid a game with less than an even chance, and you should almost never deliberately stretch to a doubtful game. You risk a *bottom* by playing in a contract no other pair will reach.

Suppose, desperate for a good score, you bid 3 NT with 23 HCP. The opponents get off to a poor defense, and the contract makes. You are vulnerable, so you score 600 — a matchpoint top. The problem is, you probably would have gotten the same top if you have played *2 NT* and made nine tricks. Plus *150* would have beaten all the other pairs, since they got better defense and were held to, at best, 120. By pushing to game, you took a needless risk. Remember, your aim is to outscore the other pairs. Bidding game may or may not be necessary.

♠ Q 10 5 3
♡ 6 5
◇ K 5
♣ K Q 9 5 4

Your partner opens 1♡, you respond 1♠, he rebids 2♡. You might try 2 NT at rubber bridge — game is still possible. Pass at matchpoints. Your chances for game do not justify jeopardizing your likely plus in 2♡.

Of course, none of this means that you should be *too* conservative. Let's face it, when you are competing against a room full of people, you need lots of good scores to come out on top. You will have to show some enterprise. You seldom get a really good score for staying out of a reasonably attractive game — even if the game turns out to be only a fair proposition, poor defense will let it make at many tables. To win at duplicate, you may have to benefit from some of that poor defense, so if you think game will be a good gamble, bid it. Just don't stretch to games that are clearly shots in the dark.

At matchpoints, players tend to open the bidding a little lighter than at other forms of bridge. As we said, a successful partscore can earn a top as easily as a grand slam, so you don't want to miss out on one.

| ♠ A J 7 6 | ♠ A 10 7 6 4 | ♠ K Q 9 6 4 |
| ♡ J 8 | ♡ 9 8 | ♡ K Q J 5 4 |
| ♢ K Q J 6 | ♢ A Q 7 6 5 | ♢ 5 4 |
| ♣ 7 6 5 | ♣ 4 | ♣ 4 |

Any of these hands might be passed at rubber bridge. At that form of scoring, missing a partscore is no disaster, and accurate game bidding is stressed. But these hands would probably be opened at matchpoints.

Since matchpoint players tend to open a lot of balanced 12-point hands, they usually assign a 15-17 HCP range to a 1 NT opening. If you use the traditional 16-18 range, you must open one of a suit and rebid 1 NT with 12 to 15 points. With such a wide range, accuracy becomes difficult — and accuracy in this common bidding sequence is most important. If a 1 NT opening can show as few as 15 points, then a notrump rebid shows 12 to 14 — a narrower range that is easier to work with.

The idea of trying for the biggest possible plus is seen in other situations.

♠ K 9 5 4
♡ A 5
♢ K 10 6 5
♣ K 6 5

Your partner opens 1 NT. At rubber bridge you might raise to 3 NT, confident that your extra high-card strength would safeguard the contract. 4 ♠ might be set with ruffs or a bad trump break. At matchpoints you should try Stayman and bid the game in spades if partner shows four spades. Though this may entail a slight risk, a spade contract on a 4-4 fit will probably produce more tricks than

152

notrump — you can't afford to miss the highest score. Slam-bidding decisions at matchpoints often involve the same problems that arise in game bidding: will slam be bid at other tables? In theory you should be willing to bid any slam that has better than a 50% chance. In practice, though, the weaker pairs in the game will often bid only the obvious slams. Furthermore, if the contract requires good play or a favorable opening lead, you will get a good matchpoint score for taking 12 tricks whether you are in slam or not. Therefore, if you are in doubt, it's better to err on the conservative side. Still, bidding a good slam gives you an excellent chance to pick up matchpoints on the field.

Picking out *which slam* to bid can pose matchpoint problems.

♠ A K
♡ Q 4
◇ A Q 9 6 5 2
♣ K 7 6

| Partner | You |
|---------|------|
| 1 ♡ | 3 ◇ |
| 4 ◇ | 4 NT |
| 5 ◇ | ? |

*Everybody* will bid some slam on these cards, so you should try 6 NT, which figures to be a reasonable contract. In fact, failure to bid slam in the highest-scoring strain could be especially costly on this deal. However, if you are considering slam in a situation where you feel you'll be alone, bid the *safest* one.

## II. COMPETITIVE BIDDING

This is the lifeblood of matchpoints, and the competition is fierce. The players constantly take aggressive actions, even wild chances, trying to beat the *par* result on the deal. The strategic considerations are different from rubber bridge partly because a *minus* score may be good enough for your matchpoint purposes.

♠ A K 9 6 4
♡ A 5
◇ 6 5 3
♣ K 6 5

| South | West | North | East |
|-------|------|-------|------|
| 1 ♠   | Pass | 2 ♠   | Pass |
| Pass  | 3 ◇  | Pass  | Pass |
| ?     |      |       |      |

Neither side vulnerable. At rubber bridge a pass would be reasonable. Your prospects in 3 ♠ are uncertain and you might beat 3 ◇. If your decision is wrong, it's no disaster — you lose only a partscore. At matchpoints, though, you should consider bidding. By doing so, you have *two* chances for a reasonable result. Either you make 3 ♠, +140; or you go down one or two (−50, −100) when West could have made 3 ◇ (for 110). An additional point is that not every West will reopen the bidding with 3 ◇. Many players in your seat will play 2 ♠. If nine tricks are available, you *must* bid to avoid a matchpoint disaster.

An unattractive option is to *double* 3 ◇, hoping to beat it two tricks for +300 and a probable top. Of course, doubling the opponents into game would be poor strategy at rubber bridge, since the contract might well make, for a big loss. But players take such chances routinely at matchpoints.

Look at this situation.

♠ K 9 5
♡ A 8 6 4
◇ Q 10 6 4
♣ 6 5

| South | West | North | East |
|-------|------|-------|------|
|       | Pass | 1 ♡   | 1 ♠  |
| 2 ♡   | 2 ♠  | Pass  | Pass |
| 3 ♡   | Pass | Pass  | 3 ♠  |
| ?     |      |       |      |

Both sides vulnerable. South must *double*. This would be unthinkable at rubber bridge, but at matchpoints it is mandatory. North rates to make 3 ♡, and many pairs in your direction will play a heart contract, scoring 140. What are South's options now that the opponents have bid 3 ♠?

1. Bid 4 ♡, probably down one — a *poor* score.
2. Pass 3 ♠. If it goes down one (not unlikely), North-South collect 100 but lose to the pairs scoring 140 in 3 ♡ — a *poor* score.
3. Double. If 3 ♠ is set one, North-South score *200*, for a likely *top*.

Of course, 3 ♠ doubled may *make*. But if your side could have made 3 ♡, −730 won't be much worse from the matchpoint angle than +100. You can't score worse than a bottom!

Here, South knows that his side has the majority of the high-card strength. We say the deal *belongs* to North-South, and East-West are trying to steal it for a small loss.

Suppose, on the same auction, South held

♠ 9 8 5
♡ A 8 6 4
◇ Q 10 6 4
♣ 7 5

South should pass at his last turn. The deal probably belongs to East-West, and even a game in spades could be cold.

When your opponents try to steal from you, however, punish them if possible. Don't be discouraged if they make a doubled partscore against you occasionally. At matchpoints it's only one bad score, and you can get bad scores just as easily by selling out to the opponents when the hand belongs to you.

Note that the opponents were vulnerable on this deal, so a one-trick set doubled would be worth *200*, an important number at duplicate because it beats the score available by declaring almost any partscore contract.

The vulnerability affects your strategy on other occasions.

Vul: N-S      ♠ Q 6
              ♡ A 7 6
              ◇ A 10 6 5
              ♣ K 10 3 2

| South | West | North | East |
|-------|------|-------|------|
|       |      | 1 ♠   | 2 ♣  |
| ?     |      |       |      |

At rubber bridge or IMPs you would double for penalties. You rate to collect at least 500, and game your way, though likely, is not certain. The odds surely favor taking the penalty. At matchpoints, bid 3 NT. This contract usually will make, and you would have to hold 2 ♣ doubled to just four tricks to earn a better score. If you are +500 against 2 ♣ doubled, you would get a matchpoint zero if the other pairs scored +600 or more declaring 3 NT.

Vul: N-S      ♠ K J 5 4
              ♡ A 7 6
              ◇ K 10 5 4
              ♣ A 5

| South | West | North | East |
|-------|------|-------|------|
|       |      |       | 1 ♡  |
| Double | 4 ♡ | 4 ♠  | Pass |
| Pass  | 5 ♡  | Pass  | Pass |
| ?     |      |       |      |

The opponents seem to have uncovered a good save, so you should be inclined to bid on, trying to get back to even with the other N-S pairs. You have a fine hand, and partner has encouraged you to try 5 ♠ by passing the save around instead of doubling. At rubber bridge you would take what you could get from 5 ♡ doubled instead of speculating with 5 ♠.

The full deal could be:

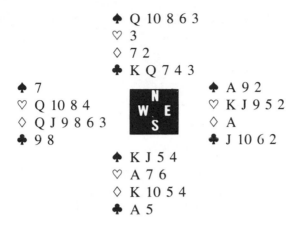

♠ Q 10 8 6 3
♥ 3
♦ 7 2
♣ K Q 7 4 3

♠ 7
♥ Q 10 8 4
♦ Q J 9 8 6 3
♣ 9 8

♠ A 9 2
♥ K J 9 5 2
♦ A
♣ J 10 6 2

♠ K J 5 4
♥ A 7 6
♦ K 10 5 4
♣ A 5

On this layout North can make 5 ♠, while East is probably down 500 in 5 ♥ doubled.

Even though a 500 sacrifice can get you a complete top if everyone else concedes −620 with your cards, you should still avoid a sacrifice unless it is fairly obvious. The problem with sacrifices is that they assume that most of the pairs in the other direction will reach game and make it. If one or two do not, the odds in your favor shrink. Don't save against a game the opponents bid hesitantly, and don't save against a game you push them into.

If you sacrifice and the opponents bid on, *let them play undoubled.* If they go down, doubled or not, your sacrifice will have done its work and your matchpoint score will be high. *If you double* and they make the contract, *you may convert a near-average score into a bottom.* Some pairs will *not* sacrifice with your cards — their opponents will play peacefully at game, scoring an overtrick. It's a case of *heads we win, tails we tie* when you push the opponents up a level with a sacrifice. Be satisfied with those odds.

The idea of seeking a very small edge is an important part of this area of matchpoints. Look at this deal.

    ♠ A 3
    ♡ 6 5 4
    ◇ A J 10 8
    ♣ K 6 5 4

    ♠ K 5
    ♡ A K 8 2
    ◇ 9 4 3
    ♣ A Q 7 3

You are declarer in 3 NT. This is a *normal contract* — every pair that holds these cards will reach the same spot, so you must pick up your edge in the play. That means you must take as many tricks as possible, even risking your contract if you judge that the odds are favorable.

Suppose West leads the ♣ Q. You win and test the clubs, finding a 3-2 split. Next you lead a diamond to dummy's jack, losing to East's queen. A spade comes back, and you win. When you lead your ◇ 9, West plays low. At rubber bridge, where making your contract is the goal, you would take the ◇ A and be satisfied with nine tricks. At matchpoints you let the ◇ 9 ride. If East wins, you will be down in a cold game. But your objective is not to make game but to beat the other pairs in 3 NT. The second diamond finesse will work about two-thirds of the time, allowing you to take two overtricks. You can't afford to ignore those odds.

Safety plays are seldom appropriate at matchpoints. When you need to take the maximum number of tricks, a safety play is a luxury you can't afford.

♠ A 4
♡ A 6 5 4
◇ 6 5 4
♣ K 9 5 4

♠ K Q 6 5
♡ 8 7 3
◇ A K
♣ A J 3 2

You are declarer in 3 NT against a diamond lead. This is another normal contract, so you must take your best play for the maximum number of tricks. At rubber bridge or IMPs, you can assure three club tricks (and nine in all) by playing the ♣ A and a club, intending to put in dummy's nine if the opponents follow with low clubs. At matchpoints you lead a spade to dummy and a club to your jack, taking your best play for four club tricks and a precious overtrick.

The time for safety is when just making your contract will give you a fine score. If you are doubled or if you have bid a game that no other pair will reach, you can play safe.

♠ 7 6
♡ J 5
◇ 7 6 4
♣ A K Q 8 6 3

♠ A Q 2
♡ 10 9 6 3
◇ A K 8 3
♣ 5 2

After two passes East opened 2 ♠. You, South, risked a takeout double. North responded with a 3 ♠ cuebid, and you tried 3 NT. All passed, and West led the ♠ 9 to your queen. How do you play?

This is an excellent contract that not many of your counterparts will reach. Your double was far from clear, as was your partner's decision to cuebid instead of jumping in clubs. It may be a good time to play safe for nine tricks. Lead a club at trick two and play low from dummy. By ensuring your contract even against a 4-1 club split, you will get a very fine matchpoint result indeed.

♠ 7 6
♡ 7 6 5
◇ K 10 7 6 4
♣ A K 10

♠ K Q
♡ A Q J 10
◇ Q J 3
♣ J 8 7 6

You, South, opened 1 NT and North raised to 3 NT. Again, the contract is normal. West leads the ♠4. East wins the ace and returns the two to your king, as West follows with the three. **How do you play?**

At rubber bridge you would go all out to make the contract by taking consecutive finesses in clubs and hearts, hoping for four tricks in each suit. But this plan is clearly against the odds, and the most likely result is an extra undertrick. At matchpoints knock out the ◇ A and settle for down one. Again, remember your aim: to beat the other pairs.

♠ K 10 5
♡ 7 6 5 4
◇ K 5
♣ A 10 3 2

♠ A J 9 8 4
♡ A Q
◇ A 9 8
♣ 7 6 5

You open 1 NT, and partner responds 3 NT. West leads a low heart, East puts up the king and you win. **Do you think this contract is normal?** It is abnormal. Many South players will open 1 ♠ and reach 4 ♠. They will lose two clubs and possibly a spade. The normal way to play the spade suit is to cash the king and finesse the jack, so if East has the ♠ Q, they will make five. Since you can never make 5 NT, you are slated for a poor score if East has the ♠ Q. You might as well play West for it by taking a (first-round) finesse through him. If this works, you'll take ten tricks and beat the pairs in 4 ♠, who will also take ten tricks.

```
        ♠ J 10 5
        ♡ 6 5 4
        ◇ A Q 5 4
        ♣ J 10 4

        ♠ A K Q 9 6 3
        ♡ A 9
        ◇ 3
        ♣ Q 9 6 3
```

| South | West | North | East |
|-------|------|-------|------|
| 1 ♠ | Pass | 2 ♠ | Pass |
| 4 ♠ | (All Pass) | | |

West leads the ♣K, continues a low club to East's ace and ruffs the club return. Next the ♡Q is led. **Plan the play.**

West's terrific lead puts you behind the 8-ball. No one else will get this defense, and game will make easily at most tables. To get back to even, you must risk the diamond finesse to get a discard for your heart loser.

You will be down two instead of one if the ◇K is wrong, but this won't affect your matchpoint result much. If you go down one, you can expect a zero.


## IV. DEFENSE

Defense is clearly more difficult at matchpoints than at rubber bridge. In a rubber game you have a single objective: beating the contract. But at duplicate, your goal may range from squeezing out a third undertrick to holding declarer to just one overtrick. Since your score is compared with your competitors' scores, every trick may be important. You can't afford to relax even when the fate of the contract is certain.

161

```
            ♠ Q 10 4
            ♡ K 5
            ◇ K Q J 10 4
            ♣ 7 6 5
♠ 8 6 3 2
♡ A 9 4 2          ┌─────────┐
◇ 5                │    N    │
♣ K 10 4 2         │  W   E  │
                   │    S    │
                   └─────────┘
```

| South | West | North | East |
|-------|------|-------|------|
| 1 ♠ | Pass | 2 ◇ | Pass |
| 2 ♣ | Pass | 3 ♠ | (All Pass) |

You, West, choose an attacking low-club lead. Partner produces the ace and continues with the queen and jack, declarer following. At rubber bridge, overtake the third club and lead a low heart. Declarer surely holds the high spades and the ◇ A for his opening bid, so your only chance to *beat* the contract is that South lacks the ♡ Q and misguesses. At matchpoints, however, you should *cash* your ace, satisfied to hold the hand to three. Your aim is not to beat the contract, but to beat the other pairs, who in all likelihood will defend the same 3 ♠ contract. At many tables the opening lead will be less inspired than yours. They may try the singleton diamond, lead a trump or lay down the ♡ A and switch to a diamond. In any case, declarer will make four or five. Your fine opening lead has earned you a good score on this deal already. It would be overkill to underlead your ♡ A. If declarer put the king up, you would never get your heart trick, and your hard-won advantage would disappear.

```
            ♠ A Q 3 2
            ♡ 9 6 5
            ◇ Q J
            ♣ J 10 9 4
♠ K 7
♡ A K 8 4 2        ┌─────────┐
◇ 10 6             │    N    │
♣ K 8 6 2          │  W   E  │
                   │    S    │
                   └─────────┘
```

| South | West | North | East |
|-------|------|-------|------|
|  | 1 ♡ | Pass | 2 ♡ |
| Pass | Pass | Double | 3 ♡ |
| 3 ♠ | Pass | 4 ♠ | |

North-South vulnerable. You, West, lead the ♡A. Your partner plays low, and declarer drops the queen. That must be a singleton, since partner wouldn't reraise to 3♡ with three low hearts, nor would South try 3♠ with two heart losers plus bad spades. The appearance of dummy is discouraging, and not just because your ♠K is a loser. Not every North will reopen the bidding, and *nobody* will raise 3♠ to 4♠. Since no other North-South pair will reach game, you will get a zero if the contract is made. You therefore must defend rubber-bridge style and try to beat it. Your best hope is that partner has the doubleton ♣A, leaving declarer with a hand like:

> ♠ J 10 9 5 4
> ♡ Q
> ◇ A K 9 4
> ♣ Q 7 3

You can take four tricks with a low club shift and a subsequent ruff. It is true that a club shift could cost an overtrick if declarer's hand is:

> ♠ 10 9 8 6 4
> ♡ Q
> ◇ K 9 4 2
> ♣ A Q 7

but that is irrelevant — your matchpoint result will be the same whether they make four or five.

# SUMMARY

*Duplicate bridge* is the type of bridge played in tournaments. At *matchpoints*, the most common form of duplicate, each deal is played *several* times under exactly *duplicated* conditions. This allows for a comparison of results after the game is over, and the winners are the pair who *made the most* of the cards they held on each deal.

Scoring at duplicate is similar to that used in *Chicago*. An arbitrary bonus is awarded for making a game or partscore and added to the trick score:

| | |
|---|---:|
| For making a vulnerable game | 500 |
| For making a non-vulnerable game | 300 |
| For making a partscore | 50 |

Here are some things to remember about matchpoint *strategy:*

I. *Constructive bidding*

1. Tend to play in the higher-scoring notrump and major-suit strains, especially at the game level.
2. Do not stretch to bid speculative games and slams.
3. In slam bidding choose the *safest* slam if you judge that slam will be bid at few of the other tables.
4. Tend to open the bidding a little lighter than at rubber bridge. A good partscore can earn you a *top* as easily as a good slam.

II. *Competitive bidding:*

1. On competitive partscore hands, your basic aim should be a plus score. However, if your side has more of the high-card strength, then the hand *belongs to you* — most of the pairs in your direction will be plus, so you need as big a plus as possible.
2. At the game level be more willing to push on when the opponents take a good sacrifice against your game. However, avoid sacrifices yourself except in obvious situations.

3. Be aggressive in competitive auctions, especially when not vulnerable. Be more willing to overcall only for lead-directing, competitive or nuisance value. Balance freely.

4. Always pay close attention to the vulnerability.

III. *Declarer play:*

1. In a *normal contract,* one that almost every pair will reach, choose the best play for the *maximum number of tricks.* Risk your contract for an overtrick if the odds are good.

2. Avoid standard safety plays unless just making your contract will be worth a good matchpoint score.

3. Don't hesitate to play for down one (or more) to get a good matchpoint result. In a sacrifice, plan the play on the assumption that your decision to save was correct.

4. If the opponents defend well, you may have to take chances to get back to even with the other pairs. If the opponents defend poorly and give away a trick or two, play to protect your advantage.

IV. *Defense:*

1. Your aim may range from holding declarer to just one overtrick to squeezing out a third undertrick. Try for the set you need to get a good *matchpoint* score.

2. Make defeating the contract your primary aim only if you defend a game or slam that won't be bid elsewhere.

3. If you get off to a good start on defense, play to protect your advantage.

4. Tend to make safe, passive opening leads.

**TEST YOUR COMPREHENSION OF THE MATERIAL IN THIS CHAPTER:**

I.   How many points would each of these contracts score at duplicate bridge?

a. 3 NT, making four, vulnerable.
b. 4♠, making five, not vulnerable.
c. 3♣, making four, vulnerable.
d. 3♠, making five, not vulnerable.
e. 6♣, making six, vulnerable.

II.  Partner opens 1 NT (16-18 HCP). How do you respond with each of these hands?

a.   ♠ Q                b.   ♠ K 9 7 6
     ♡ A 4 3                  ♡ A 2
     ◊ K J 8 6 5 3            ◊ K 7 6 5
     ♣ 10 6 4                 ♣ Q J 6

c.   ♠ K 5 4
     ♡ J 4
     ◊ K 10 6 5 3
     ♣ 7 6 5

You open 1♣, partner responds 3♣ (forcing). What do you say with:

d.   ♠ Q 6
     ♡ A 6 5
     ◊ J 5 4
     ♣ A K 6 5 4

Your partner opens 1 ◊, you respond 1 ♡, he rebids 1 ♠. What do you say with:

e.   ♠ K Q 4
     ♡ A 6 5 4
     ◊ 5 4
     ♣ 8 6 4 3

Your partner opens 1 ♠, you respond 1 NT, he rebids 2 ◊. What do you say with:

f.  ♠ J 10
    ♡ A 6 5 4
    ◊ Q 8 5
    ♣ 10 7 6 4

III.  a. (Neither side vulnerable)

| South | West | North | East |
|-------|------|-------|------|
| 1 ♡ | Pass | 2 ♡ | Pass |
| Pass | 3 ♣ | Pass | Pass |
| ? | | | |

What do you, South, say with:

    ♠ A 4
    ♡ A K 9 7 4
    ◊ K 6 5
    ♣ 5 4 3

b.  (Neither side vulnerable)

| South | West | North | East |
|-------|------|-------|------|
| 1 ♠ | Double | 2 ♠ | 3 ◊ |
| 3 ♠ | Pass | Pass | 4 ◊ |
| ? | | | |

What do you, South, say with:

    ♠ A K J 8 4
    ♡ A 5
    ◊ 10 8 2
    ♣ K 6 5

c.  (Neither side vulnerable)

| South | West | North | East |
|-------|------|-------|------|
|       |      | 1 ♠   | Double |
| 2 ♠   | 3 ◊  | Pass  | Pass |
| 3 ♠   | Pass | Pass  | 4 ◊ |
| ?     |      |       |      |

On the above bidding, what do you, South, say with:

♠ J 8 6 4
♡ 5
◊ K 6 5
♣ J 8 6 4 3

d.  You are vulnerable, they are not. North, your partner, opens
1 ♡, and East overcalls 2 ◊. What do you, South, say with:

♠ K J 4
♡ J 3
◊ A Q 4 3
♣ Q 10 4 3

IV.

a.

♠ K Q 6
♡ K 4
◊ Q J 5
♣ 9 7 6 5 3

♠ A J 10 3
♡ A 6
◊ K 10 4 3
♣ K Q J

You are declarer in 3 NT. West leads the ♡J. Plan the play.

168

b.

     ♠ 5 4
     ♡ 9 6 5 2
     ◇ K Q
     ♣ A 10 9 5 4

     ♠ A K
     ♡ A K 3
     ◇ J 5 4 3 2
     ♣ J 8 3

You are declarer in 3 NT. West, who is known to have exactly six spades, leads the ♠Q. Plan the play.

c.

     ♠ J 10 4 3
     ♡ K J 6 5
     ◇ A K J
     ♣ 5 4

     ♠ Q 9 2
     ♡ A Q 8 4 3
     ◇ 6
     ♣ A 8 6 2

You opened 1 ♡, North raised to 3 ♡, you went on to 4 ♡. West leads the ♠K, continues a low spade to East's ace and ruffs a third spade. Now the ♣Q is led. Plan the play.

d.

     ♠ 8 5 4 3
     ♡ K 10 4
     ◇ K 5
     ♣ A 10 3 2

     ♠ A Q
     ♡ A J 9 7 3
     ◇ A 6 2
     ♣ 6 5 4

You open 1 NT and arrive at 3 NT. The opening lead is the ♠2, East playing the king. Plan the play.

# SOLUTIONS

I.  a.  630
    b.  450
    c.  130
    d.  200
    e.  1370

II.  a.  3 NT.  Strain to play in notrump.
     b.  2♣.  If there is a spade fit, you may score more than in notrump.
     c.  Pass.  Don't stretch to a losing game.
     d.  3 NT
     e.  2♠.  Play in the major suit if possible.
     f.  2♠.  The *false preference* is right at matchpoints.

III.  a.  3♡.  This will be the winning move if they can make 3♣ *or* you can make 3♡.
      b.  Double  You expected to make 3 ♠, and the opponents are trying to steal the hand from you. Perhaps you can beat them 300 for a top. If they *make* 4 ◊, you were fated for a bad matchpoint score and the double will cost very little. *If you pass,* you guarantee yourself a poor result.
      c.  Pass.  The difference here is that *this is not your hand.* You took a chance to bid 3 ♠ and you pushed the opponents to 4 ◊. If they go down, your matchpoint score will be high.
      d.  3 NT.  If you can make game, you will have to beat them *four* tricks to score well.

IV.  a.  Knock out the ♣A, taking your best play for an overtrick in this normal contract.
     b.  Double finesse in clubs, playing for down one. You will probably go down two if you try to make the contract by playing diamonds. The fact that you can't make the contract with four club tricks is irrelevant. Your aim is to *beat the other pairs.*
     c.  West's great lead has put you at a disadvantage in this normal contract. Finesse the ◊ J, trying to get back to even.
     d.  If the ♡Q is on your right, the pairs in 4♡ will usually make five. Therefore, finesse West for the ♡Q, hoping to make 4 NT while the pairs in hearts also take ten tricks.

# Chapter 10

## MODERN CONVENTIONS AND TREATMENTS

Systems and conventions have proliferated in the past three decades, especially in tournament bridge where the players are always looking for ways to gain an edge. Pairs who use lots of conventions and treatments can enter the auction more often, describe certain hands that would be hard to handle without artificial methods and, in general, bid more accurately. In this chapter we will look at some of the more common conventions and treatments. We'll discuss their advantages and disadvantages, and you can decide which ones to adopt. Even if you don't care for any fancy conventions, you should still learn them so you will know what's going on if your opponents use them.

### I. TREATMENTS

A *treatment* is a way to assign a *natural* meaning to a bid. For instance, if you and partner decide that a double raise of opener's suit will show five-card support and 5-7 HCP, that's a *treatment;* non-standard, perhaps, but a bid that offers to play in partner's suit and therefore has a natural meaning.

**1. Opening in notrump.** How do you play your 1 NT openings? As we saw in Chapter 9, a 15-17 range is more practical at matchpoints than 16-18.

Balanced hands with *12 HCP* are frequently opened at matchpoints. If you open one of a suit and rebid 1 NT (or 2 NT, if necessary) to show a balanced 12-*15* HCP, coping with the 4-point range makes accuracy difficult in this common sequence. If a 1 NT opening can be made with 15 HCP, a notrump rebid covers only a 3-point range (12-*14* HCP), and responder will have a better idea of game prospects.

**2. How do you play your overcalls?** There are two schools of thought. One school considers overcalls as *destructive,* competitive or lead directing, and enters the auction on any hand that offers hope of achieving one of those goals. The other school views an overcall as *constructive*, a bid made to start a search for a good contract. This school has fairly strict requirements for overcalls, much as everyone has requirements for *opening* the bidding. Both sides agree that an overcall suggests a playable suit, but they disagree on what high-card and defensive values it promises.

If you play SOUND overcalls (generally, based on an opening bid or more):

> a.  Your chances of taking a heavy penalty are diminished.
> b.  Accuracy in constructive bidding is easier. Partner knows your strength.
> c.  You promise defensive values, so partner can judge more accurately in competition. Good penalty doubles are possible.
> d.  You give away less information the opponents can use to judge the bidding or play.

If you play LIGHT overcalls (which may be made with a poor hand):

> a.  You seldom lose a distributional make or a good sacrifice.
> b.  Lead direction is possible.
> c.  You enjoy more preemptive and nuisance effects.
> d.  Negative inferences are available to partner when you *don't* overcall.

Which side has the edge? Neither one, really. The best style is the one that works for you. However, regardless of your philosophy, you and your partner should be on the same wavelength.

**3. Your preempts.** Some pairs like to stick to the textbook on preemptive openings. Others believe it pays to gamble with light, ragged preempts, especially when the vulnerability is favorable. You and partner must know whether you would routinely open the following hand 3♣ (not vulnerable vs. vulnerable):

♠ 5
♡ 6 5
◊ 8 6 5 4
♣ Q J 9 7 5 2

172

**4. Five-card majors.** Many pairs have the agreement that an opening bid of 1 ♡ or 1 ♠ absolutely promises five cards or more. Such pairs must routinely open with three-card minor suits, even going so far as to open 1 ◊ on:

♠ K Q 10 3
♡ A K J 4
◊ 7 5 3
♣ J 6

(Some five-card majorities would violate their system on this hand and open in a major, but others adhere to the system strictly.) This is a more accurate style, since responder knows immediately when an eight-card major suit fit is available. However, it is less *preemptive* than the four-card major style. And you may lose a major suit occasionally when you cannot open in a strong four-card major.

**5. Limit raises.** In this treatment an immediate double raise of partner's opening bid is *not* forcing but *invitational.* A typical limit raise should be based on *primary values,* good distribution and good trump support. If partner opens 1 ♠, raise to 3 ♠ with either of these hands:

a.    ♠ K 8 6 4        b.    ♠ A 10 6 5 3
      ♡ A J 6 5                ♡ 3
      ◊ 2                        ◊ A 7 6 4
      ♣ 10 6 5 3             ♣ 8 7 4

If you have concentrated side values, or if your trump support for partner is mediocre, bid your side suit before supporting partner. Suppose partner opens 1 ♡.

c.    ♠ A Q J 5
      ♡ K 7 6 4
      ◊ 8 7 5
      ♣ 5 4

Respond 1 ♠ and raise hearts at your next turn. If partner knows you have side strength in spades, he can judge your game prospects more accurately.

173

The preemptive and descriptive benefits of limit raises (properly used) are great, and many players use this treatment.

**6. Inverted minor-suit raises.** This treatment was originally part of the Kaplan-Sheinwold system. A *single* raise of a minor-suit opening is *strong* and forcing, while a *double* raise is *weak* and preemptive. In theory, you can preempt the opponents on your weak hands while leaving more room to exchange information on your strong ones. A possible drawback is that this treatment may lead to unfamiliar sequences, and there is always the chance of a misunderstanding.

**7. When your partner overcalls 1 NT.** The meanings of some of your responses change. A jump response in a suit is invitational to game, not forcing. A cuebid of the opponents' suit is a substitute for Stayman. (You might want to bid 2 ♣ to play, but you wouldn't bid the opponents' suit to play.) With a strong hand, you can create a forcing situation by cuebidding the opponents' suit. Incidentally, it pays to bid aggressively after a 1 NT overcall. Partner's values are favorably located behind the opening bidder, and the play will go well when the location of the missing high cards is known.

West opens 1 ♡; North, your partner, overcalls 1 NT.

a.  ♠ A 5 4  
    ♡ 4 3  
    ◇ Q J 7 5 4 3  
    ♣ 7 6

Bid 3 ◇, invitational to game. To bid 3 NT, partner needs a maximum hand, or a fair hand with a good diamond fit.

b.  ♠ K J 6 5  
    ♡ 6 5  
    ◇ A 7 5 4 3  
    ♣ J 6

Bid 2 ♡. Stayman.

c.  ♠ K J 3  
    ♡ J 3  
    ◇ K 8 6 5 3  
    ♣ 10 6 5

Bid 3 NT. Be aggressive.

d.  ♠ A 3  
    ♡ 4 3  
    ◇ K Q J 9 5 3  
    ♣ A 5 4

Bid 2 ♡ and follow with a diamond bid. 6 ◇ is quite possible.

We still have some treatments to discuss, but now let's deal with some . . .

## II. CONVENTIONS

A *conventional* bid has an *unnatural* meaning, similar to a coded message. A Stayman response of 2 ♣, which has nothing to do with clubs, is an example. Good players adopt a convention when they decide that a bid's natural meaning is expendable and it is more useful to assign an *artificial* meaning.

Hundreds of conventions are currently used in tournament competition, some more than others. Adding a new convention to your system is a serious matter. First, ask yourself these questions:

| | |
|---|---|
| 1. | Does the convention work? Does it achieve results that would be impossible with natural methods, or is it simply a toy? |
| 2. | Is it easy to remember? |
| 3. | Can you do without the natural bid it replaces? |
| 4. | Do you get to use it enough to make learning it worthwhile? |

**1. STAYMAN.** Everyone plays this convention, and there are many variations. All experts agree, however, that at times using Stayman is probably unwise. For instance:

a. Don't use Stayman when your four-card major is poor.*
b. Don't use Stayman with 4-3-3-3 distribution. (There is room for debate here, since partner's hand may not be 4-3-3-3.)
c. Don't use Stayman (especially at rubber bridge or IMPs) when your hand contains extra high-card strength. In that case, you won't need the ruffing trick(s) that playing in a 4-4 major-suit fit will provide. You can probably make 3 NT on sheer power, while a ruff or a bad trump break may defeat a major-suit game.
d. Don't use Stayman when you have a lot of secondary values. These cards are better for notrump play.

Partner opens 1 NT. What do you respond on these hands?

a. ♠ 9 6 5 2
   ♡ A 7 6
   ◇ K J 5 3
   ♣ Q 4

   Raise to 3 NT. Stayman is questionable with such bad spades.

b. ♠ Q 7 6 4
   ♡ K 6 5
   ◇ Q J 6
   ♣ K 4 3

   Raise to 3 NT. Your distribution is flat and you have lots of queens and jacks.

c. ♠ K 7 6 4
   ♡ A Q 9
   ◇ K 10 5 4
   ♣ Q 3

   Raise to 3 NT. You have so many high cards that game in notrump will almost surely make. (At matchpoint scoring you might try 2♣. If you have a 4-4 spade fit, you might score 450 or 480 there, against 430 or 460 in notrump.)

———

*There are some experts who use Stayman with any four-card major, but they are in the minority. Many pages could be devoted to this discussion.

There are several variations on Stayman. Some pairs play FORC-ING STAYMAN, in which opener must keeping bidding on this auction:

| Opener | Responder |
|--------|-----------|
| 1 NT   | 2 ♣       |
| 2 ◊    | 2 ♡ /2 ♠  |

In NON-FORCING STAYMAN opener may pass on this sequence. Responder is only inviting game.

In TWO-WAY STAYMAN, both 2 ♣ *and* 2 ◊ are Stayman responses. 2 ♣ is reserved for weaker hands, while 2 ◊ is forcing to game and may initiate a slam try.

Two-way Stayman can gain in many situations. For example, it is possible to stop in 3 NT after finding a major-suit fit. On this auction:

| Opener | Responder |
|--------|-----------|
| 1 NT   | 2 ◊ (Two-way Stayman) |
| 2 ♡    | 3 ♡ (Forcing) |

opener can bid 3 NT with poor hearts and flat distribution. Alternately, he can cuebid with a suitable hand, since responder's sequence may imply interest in a heart *slam.*

Using two-way Stayman, you can reach minor-suit slam on a 4-4 fit. On this auction:

| Opener | Responder |
|--------|-----------|
| 1 NT   | 2 ◊ (Two-way Stayman) |
| 2 ♡    | 2 NT (Forcing) |

Opener can now mention another four-card suit, and a minor-suit fit may be found.

Since responder may use a 2 ◊ response on *any* strong hand, planning to bid his suit later, it is possible to play direct jumps to three of a minor suit as *preemptive* (TREATMENT) over a 1 NT opening in conjunction with two-way Stayman. This auction:

177

| Opener | Responder |
|--------|-----------|
| 1 NT | 2 ♣ |
| 2 any | 3 ♣ /3 ◇ |

is available to invite 3 NT. Opener needs a maximum hand, or a fair hand with a fit for responder's minor, to go on.

**2. BLACKWOOD, GERBER.** We won't list the basic responses to these familiar conventions. However, *if you must respond to Blackwood with a void:*

Bid six of your void suit (if it ranks below the agreed trump suit) with one ace and a void.

Bid six of the agreed suit (if you can't afford to show your void suit) with one ace and a void.

Bid 5 NT with two aces and a void.

You may use your judgment and decline to show a void if you feel that your void is not a feature partner will find useful.

*If the opponents interfere with a bid over partner's 4 NT inquiry,* there are several common methods. In one of them, called DOPI (pronounced "dopey"), you *double* with *no* aces, *pass* with *one* and *bid the next higher suit* with *two.*

Most pairs use *Gerber* only over an opening or first response in notrump. Any other time, 4 ♣ is too valuable as a natural call.

In KEY CARD BLACKWOOD, there is a different scheme of responses to 4 NT, with the king of the agreed trump suit counted as a fifth ace. The most common method is:

| | |
|---|---|
| 5 ♣ | 0 or 3 key cards |
| 5 ◇ | 1 or 4 |
| 5 ♡ | 2 without the queen of the agreed trump suit. |
| 5 ♠ | 2 with the queen. |

In ROMAN BLACKWOOD the responses identify *which* aces responder holds. The responses are:

| | |
|---|---|
| 5 ♣ | 0 or 3 aces |
| 5 ◇ | 1 or 4 |
| 5 ♡ | 2 aces; same color, or both majors, or both minors. |
| 5 ♠ | 2 aces; clubs and hearts, or spades and diamonds. |

Whether you use one of these variations or stick with the original article, remember that it is appropriate to take control of the auction with Blackwood only if you can place the contract accurately with the information that the response will provide. Otherwise, make your slam decision in some other way.

**3. TRANSFERS (JACOBY, TEXAS, etc.)** These are used almost exclusively in responding to a notrump opening. They force opener to *transfer* to the next higher suit. For example, a 2 ♡ response forces opener to bid 2 ♠, accepting the transfer. Transfers have two main advantages:

a. They allow the stronger hand to be declarer with his partner's suit as trumps. The defense may be more difficult with opener's high-card strength concealed, and the opening lead will come up to opener's tenaces instead of *through* them.

b. An elaborate and effective bidding system after a notrump opening bid can be built around an initial transfer.

**4. JACOBY 2 NT RESPONSE.** If you prefer *limit raises,* you must find a new *forcing* raise of partner's opening bid. One solution is to play *2 NT* as a *forcing* raise of partner's *major*-suit opening. (Forcing raises in the *minors* are less common and may be handled in some other way.) If you use this convention, you lose 2 NT as a natural response. The loss is not serious, however, since a temporizing response in a new suit is satisfactory on many hands.

Using 2 NT as a forcing major-suit raise *saves room* in the bidding. Opener rebids according to the following scheme:

| | Opener | Responder |
|---|---|---|
| | 1 ♠ | 2 NT (forcing raise). |
| | | |
| | 3 ♣ = | singleton club. |
| | 3 ◇ = | singleton diamond. |
| Opener's | 3 ♡ = | singleton heart. |
| rebids | 3 ♠ = | slam interest, no singleton. |
| | 4 ♣/4 ◇/4 ♡ = | a long suit or a void suit, according to your preference. |
| | 4 ♠ = | signoff in game. |

Some pairs use *3 NT* as a forcing major-suit raise, since 3 NT is seldom used as a natural response. However, 3 NT costs valuable bidding space.

**5. SPLINTER RESPONSES.** Unusual jumps that show a good hand, an excellent fit for partner's suit and *shortness* in the bid suit. Respond 4♣ to partner's 1♡ opening on:

♠ A J 4
♡ A 9 6 4 2
◊ K 6 5 4
♣ 4

Splinters show slam interest based on distribution more than great high-card strength. The idea is that partner can evaluate the mesh of the high cards and distribution by looking at his values opposite the short suit. For example, opener's hand might be:

♠ Q 5
♡ K Q 8 5 3
◊ A Q 8
♣ 8 5 3

Responder's splinter bid lets opener visualize the perfect fit, and the reasonable slam may be reached.

Suppose your hand is:

♠ 4
♡ A 7 6
◊ A Q 8 5 3
♣ K J 7 6

Partner opens 1◊. Jump to 3♠, showing a forcing diamond raise with spade shortness. Partner can evaluate slam prospects (or 3 NT prospects) accurately. Note that you need sound high-card values for a splinter bid over a minor-suit opening, since partner may wish to bid 3 NT. Over a *major*-suit opening, however, 11 or 12 HCP are enough — a splinter response, in fact, should deny much more in high cards. This is a slam try based on a distributional *fit*, remember.

Most of the time, splinter responses cost little. You lose the ability to preempt over partner's opening bid, which is useful on some hands. The other drawbacks are:

---

a. The opponents may double the splinter bid to indicate a safe lead or find a suit in which to sacrifice.

b. Many partnerships fail to distinguish whether a splinter bid is appropriate with a *void* suit or a singleton ace.

---

**6. FORCING 1 NT RESPONSE.** Opener *must rebid* if responder bids 1 NT over a *major*-suit opening. (Opener occasionally must rebid in a *three*-card minor suit.) The forcing 1 NT response is usually played as part of a style where a new-suit response at the two level is *forcing to game* (TREATMENT). Responder must therefore start with 1 NT on all invitational hands, a possible drawback since he cannot bid a suit to show concentrated side strength. Also, the partnership cannot play in 1 NT, often a *good matchpoint contract*. However, the *two-over-one-game-force* style allows leisurely, accurate auctions on game and slam hands, and the forcing 1 NT response works well when you pick up

♠ 5 3
♡ J 10 9 6 5 3 2
◇ A 7 4
♣ 7

and partner opens 1 ♠. You can respond 1 NT, knowing opener must rebid, and you will get to show your heart suit. With Standard methods, you risk a ludicrous result on this hand.

If you adopt this style, you and partner must discuss your methods thoroughly. When you play an unfamiliar system, there is more chance of a damaging misunderstanding.

**7. DRURY.** A *2 ♣ response* to a third or fourth seat opening bid, conventionally asking whether the opening was made on sub-minimum values. In the original version a 2 ◇ rebid by opener said he had opened light. Now there are several variations. If your partners often open ragged hands in third and fourth position, you can adopt Drury to protect yourself and keep from getting too high.

**8. FLANNERY.** A popular convention. Flannery is a *2 ◇* opening to show a hand with five (rarely, more than five) hearts and four

181

spades! There are various problems in describing these hands, some of which Flannery seeks to overcome. For instance, responder no longer has to bid 1 ♠ over a 1 ♡ opening with four bad spades (risking a raise with only three-card support by opener, who is anxious to play in a major suit). Opener denies four spades if he opens 1 ♡ (unless he has the values to reverse).

Continuing the auction, responder can bid 2 NT over 2 ◊ to ask opener for more information about his strength (Flannery is normally used with hands in the 11-15 HCP range) and distribution.

Flannery has several advantages and drawbacks. It is possible, for example, to reach good distributional games. However, opener sometimes has trouble describing his suit quality and the location of his high-card strength, and responder must choose a contract without that knowledge.

**9. GAMBLING 3 NT OPENING.** Since most pairs can describe a *balanced* 25-27 HCP by starting with a 2 ♣ opening, a 3 NT *opening* can have a different meaning. Many pairs use it to show a solid seven-card minor suit that will produce most of the tricks for 3 NT. (According to partnership agreement, opener may or may not have cards outside his minor.) Responder may pass if he thinks 3 NT will make; otherwise, he can run to 4 ♣. Opener converts to 4 ◊ if that is his suit.

**10. LANDY.** A *2 ♣* overcall of the opponents' 1 NT opening, used to show length in both major suits (usually ten or more cards, sometimes only nine, but almost always with five or more hearts.) The ability to show two-suited hands is often desirable (especially if you have the major suits). You will take lots of tricks if partner has support for either of your suits. Several similar conventions — RIPSTRA, BECKER, ASTRO and BROZEL — show specific two-suiters over the opponents' 1 NT opening.

**11. MICHAELS CUEBID.** A direct cuebid of an opponent's opening bid has traditionally shown a hand worth a forcing two-bid. But the chance to use a cuebid like that almost never comes along, so many players have given another meaning to a direct cuebid. In Michaels, a direct cuebid shows a weakish two-suited (rarely, three-suited) hand, typically 5-5 or better. Over a minor-suit opening, you promise length in both majors. Over a major-suit opening, you promise length in the other major plus a minor. Partner can bid 2 NT to find out which minor suit you have.

**12. UNUSUAL NOTRUMP.** Over an opposing opening bid, a *jump in notrump* shows a weakish hand with length in both *minor* suits (or in the two lower unbid suits, if the opening bid was in a minor). Invariably, you have ten or more cards in your suits. The bid may also be used in situations when an overcall in notrump could not be strength-showing — for instance, when you are a passed hand.

*Note this well:* In principle, gadgets that show two-suiters suggest a hand that is *sacrifice-oriented.* A typical holding is K-Q-J-x-x in one suit, Q-J-10-x-x in the other. You have playing tricks but little defensive strength. (With a better hand in high cards, bid one of your suits and bid the other one at your next turn.) You may make an exception when (a) the vulnerability is unfavorable and a sacrifice is unlikely, or (b) when you have a huge hand and plan to cuebid or force to game later.

Conventions such as Landy, Michaels and the Unusual Notrump should not be used indiscriminately. *They give away information about your hand if an opponent becomes declarer.*

**13. NEGATIVE DOUBLES.** This is one of the most widely-played conventions, for several good reasons:

| | |
|---|---|
| 1. | It is effective. |
| 2. | It is simple. |
| 3. | Little is lost by using it. Penalty doubles are still possible. |
| 4. | You can use it often. |

When your pair uses negative doubles, many low-level doubles are played for *takeout.* This lets you enter the auction as responder with certain hands on which no *bid* is right.

This chart suggests what a negative double should promise in some common sequences.

If the auction goes:

| North | East | South | South should hold: |
|-------|------|-------|--------------------|
| 1♣ | 1◇ | Double | 6+ HCP, both four-card majors. |
| 1♣/1◇ | 1♡ | Double | 6+ HCP, four spades, plus length in the other minor or support for partner's minor. (Therefore, a 1♠ bid by South would promise five or more spades, or, rarely four very strong ones.) |
| 1♣/1◇ | 1♠ | Double | 7+ HCP and four hearts, *or* less than 10 HCP and five or more hearts. If your hand is weak, you need a *landing place*: support for partner's minor, length in the other minor, or lots of hearts. |
| 1◇ | 2♣ | Double | 8+ HCP, length in both majors. Could be 4-4 with 8+ HCP, or 5-4 (or 4-5) with 8-11 HCP. Conceivably, South could have just one major, particularly spades, and some diamond support, but troubles can arise in this style. |
| 1♡ | 1♠ | Double | 10 HCP or less. Length in both minors or just in diamonds. |
| 1♣/1◇ | 2♡ | Double | 8+ HCP with four spades and a landing place, or 8-11 HCP with five or more spades. |
| 1♡ | 2♣ | Double | 9+ HCP, length in both minors, or a lot of diamonds, or heart tolerance plus a minor. |
| 1♣/1◇ | 2♠ | Double | 9+ HCP with four hearts and a landing place, or 8-11 HCP with five or more hearts. |
| 1♠ | 2♡ | Double | 9+ HCP, length in both minors, or a lot of diamonds, or spade support plus a minor. |
| 1♡ | 3♣ | Double | 9-12 HCP with five or more spades plus a landing place, or 10+ HCP with four spades plus a landing place. |

This chart shows a possible range for negative doubles, but it would not meet with the approval of every expert. Some players, for example, refuse to make *one-suit* negative doubles — they would always have both unbid suits.

Most partnerships use negative doubles only through the three level.

*Rebidding after partner's negative double:* Basically, you rebid as if partner bid the suit or suits his negative double shows. In this auction, for example:

| South | West | North | East |
|-------|------|-------|------|
| 1 ♣ | 1 ♡ | Double | Pass |
| 2 ♠ | | | |

South's bidding suggests a minimum hand with four spades. South might rebid *1 ♠* here with only *three* spades. A 2 ◊ rebid would *not* be a reverse (promising extra strength), only an attempt to place the contract unless responder is very strong. A jump rebid by opener is game-invitational. With a strong hand opener can create a forcing situation by cuebidding overcaller's suit.

Opener should *seldom pass* a negative double for penalty. Responder will not expect this action, and his hand may be very distributional and ill-suited to defense. You need a sound holding in overcaller's suit to convert a low-level negative double for penalty.

*Reopening the auction:* It is a popular myth that you *must* reopen the auction if an opponent's overcall is passed back to you, partner having failed to act. If chances seem reasonable that partner had to pass with a penalty double of the overcall, you may reopen with a double, hoping partner can pass. (Partner is less likely to trap pass if vulnerable against not vulnerable.) However, you should not distort your hand by doubling just because partner *may* have a penalty double. Don't go headhunting.

**14. RESPONSIVE DOUBLES** show (generally) the unbid suits after partner overcalls or makes a takeout double, and the opponents compete.

| South | West | North | East |
|-------|------|-------|------|
| 1 ♡ | 2 ♣ | 2 ♡ | Double |

East has something like

♠ K J 7 5
♡ 7 6
◊ K 9 6 4 3
♣ Q 6

185

He has enough cards to act, but no bid stands out. Responsive doubles are useful in handling certain awkward hands, and little is lost by using them — it is seldom lucrative to double the opponents for penalty at the two level when they have a decent trump fit.

Conventions and treatments are fun to play and they can improve your results. However, the conventions and treatments we discussed are *optional.*. Indeed, you shouldn't bother with them if they will be confusing or hard to remember. Many successful pairs keep the gadgets to a minimum, and there are better ways to become a winner at bridge than to play a lot of conventions. If you do decide to use one of these special methods, be sure that you and your partner discuss it thoroughly in advance.

---

## SUMMARY

Pairs who employ bidding conventions and treatments can get into the auction more often, describe hands that would be awkward without artificial methods, and in general conduct auctions that are more comfortable and precise.

A TREATMENT is a way of assigning a *natural* meaning to a bid.

A CONVENTION is a bid with an *unnatural* meaning, like a coded message. Players adopt a convention when they decide that a bid's natural meaning is expendable and it is more useful to assign the bid an artificial meaning.

Before adopting a convention, ask yourself these questions:

> 1. Does the convention work? Does it achieve results that would be impossible using natural methods, or is it simply a toy?
> 2. Is it easy to remember?
> 3. Can you live without the natural bid it replaces?
> 4. Do you get to use it enough to make learning it worth the trouble?

Any convention or treatment is *optional.* Do not use a convention that is confusing. If you do adopt a convention, you and your partner should discuss it thoroughly before you play.

**TEST YOUR COMPREHENSION OF THE MATERIAL IN THIS CHAPTER:**

I.    You are playing *limit raises* — an immediate double raise of partner's opening bid shows *invitational* strength. What do you respond on these hands when partner opens 1 ♡?

    a.    ♠ A J 4 3        b.    ♠ A Q J 7
            ♡ K J 7 6                ♡ K 6 5 4
            ♢ 4                      ♢ 6 5 4
            ♣ 9 8 7 5                ♣ 5 4

    c.    ♠ 5 4               d.    ♠ 2
            ♡ K Q 3                  ♡ K Q 5 4
            ♢ 8 7 6                  ♢ 6 5 4
            ♣ A J 7 6 5            ♣ A 7 6 5 4

    e.    ♠ Q 4 3
            ♡ K J 6 5
            ♢ Q 6 5
            ♣ Q 5 4

II.   Left-hand opponent opens 1 ♢ , partner overcalls 1 NT. What do you do with these hands?

    a.    ♠ K J 3 2        b.    ♠ 9 7 6
            ♡ A Q 5 4              ♡ A 3 2
            ♢ 3 2                   ♢ J 10
            ♣ 4 3 2                 ♣ K 10 7 5 3

    c.    ♠ A 5 4           d.    ♠ A 5 4
            ♡ 5 4                   ♡ A 5 4
            ♢ 5 4                   ♢ 5
            ♣ Q J 9 6 5 4         ♣ K Q 8 6 5 4

    e.    ♠ 7 6 5
            ♡ Q 7 6
            ♢ 4
            ♣ J 9 6 5 4 3

III.    Your partner opens 1 NT. With which of these hands do you employ the Stayman convention?

a.    ♠ 10 6 5 4        b.    ♠ A 6 5 4
      ♡ A J 5                  ♡ J 8 7
      ◊ A Q 4 2                ◊ A J 2
      ♣ J 10                   ♣ 10 5 4

c.    ♠ Q 9 6 5        d.    ♠ K 7 6 4
      ♡ Q 10 4                ♡ A Q 6
      ◊ Q J                   ◊ K 5 4 3
      ♣ K J 10 2              ♣ Q J

e.    ♠ A J 4 3
      ♡ 4 3
      ◊ A J 7 6
      ♣ 6 5 4

IV.    You and partner agree on hearts as trumps, and he bids 4 NT, Blackwood. How do you respond with these hands?

a.    ♠ A 5 4 3        b.    ♠ —
      ♡ K J 7 6                ♡ K J 7 6
      ◊ —                      ◊ Q 7 6 5 4
      ♣ Q 7 6 5 4             ♣ A 6 5 4

c.    ♠ A 6 5 4
      ♡ K J 6 5
      ◊ —
      ♣ A 7 6 5 4

V.    You and partner agree on hearts as trumps. He bids 4 NT, Blackwood, and your right-hand opponent interferes with 5 ♣. You have agreed to use DOPI over interference. What do you do with these hands?

a.    ♠ K J 5 4        b.    ♠ A 6 5 4
      ♡ A 6 5 4                ♡ A 7 6 5
      ◊ 8 7 6                  ◊ K Q
      ♣ K Q                    ♣ 6 5 4

188

VI.    With neither side vulnerable, RHO opens 1♠. With which of these hands would you employ the Unusual Notrump?

a.  ♠ 5 4
    ♡ 3
    ◊ A K 6 5 4
    ♣ A Q 4 3 2

b.  ♠ —
    ♡ A Q 5
    ◊ K 7 6 5
    ♣ Q J 10 6 5 4

c.  ♠ —
    ♡ J 7
    ◊ K Q 10 7 6
    ♣ Q J 9 7 6 5

d.  ♠ A Q
    ♡ —
    ◊ K Q J 6 5
    ♣ A K 10 6 5 4

e.  ♠ A 3
    ♡ A
    ◊ J 9 7 6 5
    ♣ Q 8 6 5 4

VII.   Partner opens 1◊, and your RHO overcalls 1♠. Which of these hands is suitable for a negative double?

a.  ♠ 4 3
    ♡ K Q 6 5
    ◊ K 5 4 2
    ♣ 6 5 4

b.  ♠ 7 6
    ♡ K 8 5 3 2
    ◊ A 7 6
    ♣ J 5 4

c.  ♠ 5 4
    ♡ A J 6 5
    ◊ J 7 2
    ♣ A K 6 5

d.  ♠ A 3 2
    ♡ K Q 7 6 5
    ◊ Q 4 3
    ♣ 4 3

VIII.  You open 1♡, LHO overcalls 1♠, partner makes a negative double. What do you rebid with these hands?

a.  ♠ A Q
    ♡ A K J 7 6
    ◊ K 6 5
    ♣ J 6 5

b.  ♠ A 7 6
    ♡ A K 7 6 5
    ◊ 7
    ♣ J 7 6 5

c.  ♠ A 5
    ♡ A K 6 5 4
    ◇ 5 4
    ♣ A J 5 4

d.  ♠ A
    ♡ A K 6 5 4
    ◇ A Q 6 5
    ♣ K 5 4

e.  ♠ Q J 9 5
    ♡ A Q 6 5 4
    ◇ K 6
    ♣ J 7

IX.  You open 1 ♠, LHO overcalls 2 ◇, passed back to you. You are using negative doubles, and neither side is vulnerable. What do you do with these hands?

a.  ♠ A K 9 8 2
    ♡ K 7
    ◇ Q J 8 7
    ♣ 7 6

b.  ♠ A Q 7 6 5
    ♡ K 7 6
    ◇ 8 7
    ♣ A J 6

c.  ♠ A Q 8 7 6
    ♡ A K Q 7
    ◇ —
    ♣ A J 7 6

d.  ♠ K J 7 6 5
    ♡ K J
    ◇ 8 7 6
    ♣ A 7 6

e.  ♠ A K Q 7 6 5
    ♡ 7 3
    ◇ K 7
    ♣ K 6 5

## SOLUTIONS

I.   a.  3 ♡
     b.  1 ♠.  Show your concentrated side strength.
     c.  2 ♣.  Temporize with only three-card heart support.
     d.  3 ♡
     e.  2 ♡,  all this hand is worth
II.  a.  2 ◇,  Stayman
     b.  3 NT,  aggressive
     c.  3 ♣,  invitational
     d.  2 ◇,  heading for 6 ♣
     e.  2 ♣,  natural here

| III. | a. | no, | bad spades (but some experts bid 2♣) |
| | b. | no, | flat distribution (but this is a judgment call) |
| | c. | no, | too many secondary values |
| | d. | no, | ample high-card strength to make game in notrump on power |
| | e. | yes | |
| IV. | a. | 6◊, | one ace and a diamond void |
| | b. | 6♡, | one ace and a spade void |
| | c. | 5 NT, | two aces and a void |
| V. | a. | Pass, | one ace |
| | b. | 5◊, | two aces |
| VI. | a. | no, | too much defense. Overcall 2◊. |
| | b. | no, | wrong pattern and too much defense. Overcall 2♣. |
| | c. | yes | |
| | d. | yes, | planning to bid a lot more later |
| | e. | no, | the suit quality is terrible. You have no playing tricks. |
| VII. | a. | yes | |
| | b. | yes | |
| | c. | yes | |
| | d. | no. | Bid 2♡. |
| VIII. | a. | 2 NT, | inviting game |
| | b. | 2♣ | |
| | c. | 3♣, | inviting game |
| | d. | 2♠, | suggesting a strong hand |
| | e. | 1 NT. | Do not pass. |
| IX. | a. | Pass. | Partner cannot have diamonds and did not raise spades or make a negative double. |
| | b. | Double | |
| | c. | 3◊ | |
| | d. | Pass, | too weak to risk a second bid |
| | e. | 2♠ | |

# DEVYN PRESS PUBLICATIONS
# BRIDGE BOOKS